YOUR WORRY MAKES SENSE

of related interest

The Ultimate Anxiety Toolkit
25 Tools to Worry Less, Relax More, and Boost Your Self-Esteem
Risa Williams
Illustrated by Jennifer Whitney and Amanda Way
ISBN 978 1 78775 770 7
eISBN 978 1 78775 771 4

The Anxiety Recovery Journal
Creative Activities to Keep Yourself Well
Cara Lisette and Anneli Roberts
Illustrated by Victoria Barron
Foreword by Annie Hickox
ISBN 978 1 80501 079 1
eISBN 978 1 80501 080 7

Turn the Tide on Climate Anxiety
Sustainable Action for Your Mental Health and the Planet
Megan Kennedy-Woodard and Dr Patrick Kennedy-Williams
Foreword by Arizona Muse – Founder and Trustee of Dirt
Foundation for the Regeneration of Earth
ISBN 978 1 83997 067 2
eISBN 978 1 83997 068 9

ACT for Burnout
Recharge, Reconnect, and Transform Burnout with
Acceptance and Commitment Therapy
Debbie Sorensen
ISBN 978 1 83997 537 0
eISBN 978 1 83997 538 7

YOUR WORRY MAKES SENSE

Anxiety and Burnout are Logical
(and You Can Overcome Them)

Dr Martin Brunet

Illustrated by Hannah Robinson

Jessica Kingsley Publishers
London and Philadelphia

First published in Great Britain in 2025 by Jessica Kingsley Publishers
An imprint of John Murray Press

1

The information contained in this book is not intended to replace the services of trained medical professionals or to be a substitute for medical advice. You are advised to consult a doctor on any matters relating to your health, and in particular on any matters that may require diagnosis or medical attention.

A CIP catalogue record for this title is available from the British Library and the Library of Congress

ISBN 978 1 80501 297 9
eISBN 978 1 80501 298 6

Printed and bound in Great Britain by Clays Ltd

Jessica Kingsley Publishers
Carmelite House
50 Victoria Embankment
London EC4Y 0DZ

www.jkp.com

John Murray Press
Part of Hodder & Stoughton Ltd
An Hachette Company

The authorised representative in the EEA is Hachette Ireland,
8 Castlecourt Centre, Dublin 15, D15 XTP3, Ireland (email: info@hbgi.ie)

Contents

For Eugene, because I know you would have been proud of me

Acknowledgements

The greatest influence on this book by far, which has determined its contents, informed its structure and shaped the stories within it, has been the education I have received from my patients at Binscombe Medical Centre. And so my greatest thanks is to you; thank you for sharing your stories, your vulnerabilities, your tears and your laughter with me. Thank you for putting up with me for running late, for those times when I haven't listened as well as I might have or have been too quick to give advice that wasn't for you. You have taught me more than I have ever learned from a textbook or a lecture, and I am truly grateful.

This book also would not have been possible if I didn't enjoy going to work, and I am so grateful to have spent most of my working life at Binscombe, a place where shared values of caring and dedication, combined with a culture of not taking ourselves too seriously, has allowed a wonderful team to flourish. I am especially grateful to my partners for being on that journey with me for so many years, and for giving me untold freedom to write and express my views.

I have loved working with Hannah Robinson as she dreamed up the illustrations for this book. At every stage, she took my ideas to another level, starting with thoughts that I could only just visualize and bringing them to life with her unique combination of drama, humour and vibrancy. Thank you so much, Hannah, I love your work! Thank you also to all the team at Jessica Kingsley Publishers, for keeping me informed at every step of the way, being so responsive to all my questions and making this book into something to be proud of. And especial thanks to Jane Evans, my editor, for combining such encouragement about my writing with insightful wisdom into how to make it better; I am truly grateful.

Lastly, I would like to thank my family for their love, care, encouragement and support. Specifically, to Joe and Katie for their social media advice, to Ellen for her insightful and meticulous proofreading, as well as for bringing Wilbur to life, and to Callum for his excellent photography skills. And always to Clare, for not just guiding me through this manuscript, but for guiding me through my life.

Introduction

When you have worked as a GP for a while, you start to notice patterns. There are patterns of illness, of course: how symptoms cluster together with certain conditions, the time of year when you see the same problems emerge, the way diseases evolve over time. You also notice patterns in what people say and how they describe their problems. If there is one thing that people affected by anxiety say to me time and time again, it is this: 'I know I'm being ridiculous, Doctor.'

People feel ridiculous or foolish for worrying about things, and the fact that they can't stop worrying makes them feel even more ridiculous. There are plenty of reasons why this might be. Often, we worry about things that we can't change. Maybe our grand-daughter is with the army and on a tour of duty close to a war zone. We worry she will come to harm. We know that this worry can't protect her and just makes us feel awful, but we can't stop ourselves. People tell us that she will be all right, that it was her dream to join the army, that she's not too close to the action, and mostly they are right, but that just makes us feel more foolish because we worry just the same.

Or maybe we worry about going out to see our friends. It makes no sense – they are our *friends* and they are always pleased to see us, they treat us kindly and tell us not to worry – and yet we do worry, and so we stay at home, feeling less anxious because we don't have to face going out. If anyone asks us to explain why we didn't go, then we make excuses, as it just sounds ridiculous to tell the truth.

Or maybe it is going to the supermarket. It's not like the shopping can hurt us, or anyone is out to harm us – people didn't even notice us when we used to go, because they were too busy with their own shopping anyway – and yet there is something about going there, to that harmless, everyday place where we always used to buy our groceries, that fills us with illogical, nonsensical, bone-shaking dread. And so we shop online and get a delivery, and we tell ourselves it's for convenience; we know that's not the case, but it just feels too foolish to say otherwise.

The problem with feeling foolish is that it only makes things worse; it disempowers us by condemning us and making us feel that *we* are the problem. *We* are at fault for worrying, *we* must have some character flaw that makes us worry, while others just get on without a care in the world. We feel ashamed, because it is so hard to talk about or explain, or because we fear how people will react when we tell them. People can be cruel when they are trying to be kind; they tell us not to worry – as if that will make it all just go away – or they even come right out with it and tell us not to be so 'stupid'.

And that is why this book is called *Your Worry Makes Sense*, because the most important thing to learn about worry is that it is not foolish or ridiculous; it is actually highly logical and makes a lot of sense. We need to learn that it is not in the least bit foolish to feel these emotions, that they have a very sensible, rational and necessary purpose, and that telling someone not to worry is like telling them not to breathe, not to be alive, not to be human. And yet anxiety can be an enormous challenge to live with, and when it gets out of control, it *appears* to make no sense at all.

I also notice patterns around the common and bewildering experience of burnout, and how profound the experience of anxiety can be when we become overwhelmed by stress. There are many root causes of anxiety, of course, and burnout may not be the main issue for you. But if you are affected by burnout, then nothing I have to say about anxiety will be of use to you until you can recognize this and start to rest and recover. Which is why such an important part of the book is the section on burnout, which I have subtitled 'You can't get better if you are running on empty'. In fact, if burnout is the reason you have picked this book up, then, after reading this introduction, I'd recommend that you jump straight to Part 2 and learn about burnout first; it works well as a stand-alone section of the book – and let's face it, you are probably too tired to read the whole book right now anyway!

The other patterns I notice in my work as a GP are the repeated patterns of what I find myself saying to my patients. There are the questions I ask again and again, because I have learned how often they reveal what is really going on when someone is affected by anxiety. Questions like 'What does your anxiety stop you doing?', 'Can you remember your first panic attack? Tell me about that,' 'What time do you turn the light out to sleep, and what time do you get up in the morning?' I ask these questions so many times because people have the same struggles, and because dealing with anxiety is like navigating a minefield. There are so many potential mistakes you can make; there are actions you take because they are so natural and obvious, and yet they trap you in a vicious cycle that gets tighter and tighter the more you do them. Things like avoiding something that scares you, or sleeping in when you've had a bad night – what could possibly be wrong with that? I'm sure that many people tiptoe successfully around these traps and make it through without any need of my help, but those who come to see me have often fallen into a pit; they don't know how they got there, and they don't know how to climb out.

I find patterns in the advice I give; indeed, I have learned that just telling people what to do is rarely successful. I need to bring someone with me: to help understand what really matters to them, what they want to change and what is off limits. I have conversations about the importance of sleep, and how to get some basic things in place to get a chance of being able to sleep well. I see patterns in the discussions I have with patients about avoidance behaviour, the need to accept fear and learn how to manage it rather than hope it won't happen, and the way thoughts, feelings and behaviours interact. I talk about how motivation wanes over time while habits strengthen, how small, successful changes are more likely to help than grand unrealistic plans and how good it is to celebrate even the smallest victories. And I have many conversations about burnout: about how bewildering it can be for the person who burns out, even though it may have been obvious to everyone else; and how you may be exactly the sort of person who is at risk of burnout, but not for the reasons you are imagining.

And that is why I had to write this book – because anxiety and burnout are so common, and mistakes are so easy to make. There is such a need out there to understand them better, both for ourselves and for those we care about who are affected by mental health problems. As a GP, I am constrained by only being with one patient at a time, and being limited by the time I have with them. There is so much more I want to say about these topics, and this book is my attempt to say it.

Your Worry Makes Sense is a GP's perspective on why anxiety happens and how it is entirely logical that it is such a common feature in our lives. I will explore how this same logic can explain why this anxiety, which is meant to protect us, can escape from its box and take on a new level where it starts to dominate and control areas of our lives. I will look at the triggers for anxiety, some of the many harmful ways we try to take anxiety away, and the more helpful techniques we can use to regain control. I will argue that we need to accept, and even appreciate, anxiety in our lives, and that there is a world of difference between feeling that anxiety is in control of us and knowing that *we* are in control of *it*. I will look at the common experience of burnout and how this can result in sudden, catastrophic anxiety – and yet by understanding it, making a few changes and giving ourselves time, how we can recover and flourish once more. And lastly, I will look at treatments for anxiety and burnout, both psychological and medical.

One of the most rewarding aspects of my job is hearing patients tell their stories, and it is in this act of listening that I have learned the most as a doctor. It therefore seemed right to incorporate stories into the text. Some of these are the direct words that have been shared with me by individuals kind enough to give me permission to reproduce their story here, some with their real name and some with their name changed; others are imagined tales based on composite stories my patients have told me over the years. I hope you find them as helpful to listen to as I have.

Part 1

Anxiety and avoidance

The safety mechanisms that tie us in knots

Chapter 1

Anxiety just wants to keep you safe

Round the Tree

When I was a child, my siblings and I invented what we thought was a truly fabulous game called 'Round the Tree'. It was played on the campsite that my family owned when I was growing up, where we lived and worked all summer. It usually took place on a quiet afternoon when all the campers had gone to the beach and left their closed-up tents as the perfect stage for our game. The action centred on a wonderful old fir tree that grew near the middle of the field, which had plenty of low-lying branches, ideal for climbing. Best of all was one strong, horizontal branch about six feet from the ground. It was easy to get to and comfortable to sit on, so much so that its bark became silky smooth from the wear it endured, as we each in turn sat astride it to play the game.

One person would be the 'looker', perched on this six-foot platform, while the others would try to go around the tree – hence our rather unimaginative title for the game! Crouched behind the tents, hidden from the view of the looker, we would attempt to dash from one tent to the next without being seen until, at last, we would be spied and our name called out. Scores would be chalked in quarter turns or half turns; occasionally, someone would even get all the way around the tree before being spotted.

The tree didn't stop at this favoured branch, and sometimes I would venture higher to another branch about three feet further on, but that was my limit; my heart would race at the thought of going higher and fear told me my limits. I am sure my parents were glad that it did.

Wouldn't it be great to never feel any fear? To be completely free of any sense of dread, anxiety or worry? To wake up in the morning with no concerns about the day, to be able to talk to anyone and do anything without anxiety, to breeze through that interview or perform on the stage without a care in the world? Or would it?

I recently read a brief summary of the remarkable life of John McAfee, the inventor of McAfee antivirus software. He lived a turbulent, highly controversial and flamboyant life, making and losing fortunes with seemingly equal ease. In 2012, when he was living in Belize, he was wanted for questioning by the police in relation to the murder of his neighbour. When the police came to his house, he was nowhere to be found, but they eventually caught up with him in Guatemala. It was expected that he would be arrested for the murder, but within a week he was released as a free man. What is remarkable is what he said sometime later: 'After it was over, I asked myself, "Good Lord, I must have been afraid?" But I really can't remember.'

We are all wonderfully different

'I really can't remember!' The police are chasing you across Central

America, wanting to question you about a murder, and you can't *remember* if you were afraid? Whatever that statement is, it is certainly not normal! It is remarkable how unafraid some people can be, but most of us would have had no trouble remembering the absolute terror we would have felt in anything like those circumstances. Maybe that is also why most of us will neither become incredibly rich nor end up being chased by the police, and why the John McAfees of this world are the exception and not the norm. Most of us do worry about things, and perhaps there are good reasons why we do.

A couple of years ago, my wife and I were fortunate enough to be able to visit Canada, and the highlight of our trip was when we went bear watching on the west coast of British Columbia. On one occasion, we were able to watch a mother grizzly bear and her triplets as they slowly wound their way up an estuary, eating up the shore crabs as they went. What was fascinating about the

cubs was how one always stayed near its mother, while another was constantly pushing the boundaries of how far it could stray; curiosity and adventure made it venture this way or that, and its mother had to keep a constant watchful eye. The third cub oscillated between the two, regularly going to see what its adventurous sibling was up to and then going back to the security of its mother.

The rangers who had taken us on the trip commented that this was what they always saw when there were three cubs. You can see why the survival of bears might be helped by this range of behaviour: the adventurous cub is more likely to get into trouble and could be the one to be harmed if danger suddenly came upon the family, but it is also more likely to survive on its own when the time comes to be independent. Nature has determined that some animals are risk takers while others are more cautious. Species thrive when there is a range, so we should not be surprised if the same is true for humans; nor should we be surprised that fear and anxiety have an important survival function.

Matthew's story

Matthew describes his experience of anxiety like this:

I'd wake early and not be able to get back to sleep, I'd have a racing heart, which I was acutely aware of – it felt like it was beating strongly. I stopped enjoying things I'd usually enjoyed, and I lacked energy and motivation. I lost my appetite, which was replaced by nausea, including retching and sometimes vomiting. I had a horrible sense of dread, like something awful was going to happen, or that I wouldn't be able to cope or get done what I needed to get done. I was often tearful. And yet, at the end of each day, often those symptoms had lifted; I had managed to get done what was needed. I noticed as I improved that the symptoms began to lift earlier in the day.

Matthew's experience of anxiety is unpleasant, and it completely dominated his life for a few months until things improved, but anxiety and fear do have a function. After all, what would it have been like if, when climbing my favourite fir tree, I had felt no fear at all? It was always fear that stopped me going higher than the upper branch, and so what would have stopped me if fear had been taken away? Would logic have been enough on its own? I might have made a rational calculation about the smaller size of the upper branches, the increasing likelihood that they wouldn't take my weight and the sure risk of injury should I fall, but, without fear, would this have been *powerful* enough to stop me? Fear has the capacity to become an extremely powerful driver, but so too do curiosity and the desire to impress. When the danger is great, it is essential that fear is sufficiently powerful that it overrides our other emotions and stops us in our tracks. If that wasn't the case, then many more children would fall out of trees, and a fair few adults as well!

What is more, anxiety does not only have a role in keeping us physically safe. If we didn't worry about how to pay the bills, we might spend recklessly and get into debt; anxiety about an upcoming exam is a powerful motivator to get down to study; worrying that our house might get burgled reminds us to lock the door when we leave home. Of course, anxiety is not the only motivator to do these things – for instance, we can prepare for an exam because we want to do well and not because we fear failure, and we usually lock the door just because it is part of our routine. The uneasy feeling anxiety leaves us with, however, can be an effective check on our behaviour, a necessary safety balance when we are in danger of doing something we might regret.

Anxiety needs to have a wide range of 'volume' in order to perform its function – from the quiet whisper of unease that makes us check if we really did close the door, to the shattering scream that stops us in our tracks when we are in mortal danger. Just as the adventurous bear cub needs to have something to hold it back from straying so far that it gets lost, so too the cub that sticks close to its mother needs to be able to overcome the fear of separation at some stage, or it will never learn to fend for itself. Anxiety, therefore, on the one hand needs to be something we can detect and recognize while consciously overriding it when we need to, and on the other must be able to so ramp up the volume that it becomes overriding fear and stops us in our tracks before we do something truly reckless.

When anxiety becomes a problem, it is usually an issue with the volume control. The level of anxiety we feel is out of proportion to the problem we are facing, or the anxiety persists longer than it needs to – sometimes never seeming to turn itself off, so that we are left with the constant hum of 'danger' being sounded in the background of our minds. Or the problem may be that the volume level is constantly being ramped up to maximum when seemingly minor triggers lead to full-blown fear, the result of which is a panic attack.

What is the purpose of a panic attack?

It is hard to understand why people have panic attacks. It is often said, quite rightly, that when we are afraid, our body releases the hormone adrenaline (also called epinephrine) and that this is the *fright, flight and fight* hormone. Our body releases it into the blood stream when we are frightened, and it helps us to run away (flight) or stand and fight if we need to. Adrenaline does this by bringing our body into a heightened state; it increases our heart rate and blood pressure, and opens the airways in our lungs so that we can deliver more oxygen to the muscles that will need them if we are to run or fight; it dilates our pupils so that we can see more clearly and releases glucose into the blood stream so that our brain has all the fuel it needs for whatever crisis is upon us. This explains many of the symptoms of anxiety – the palpitations, wide eyes and sweaty palms, for instance – and, as unpleasant as some of these symptoms are, it all makes sense because we are more likely to be able to run or defeat our assailant if we have plenty of adrenaline on board. But what is the point of a panic attack? How can I run or fight when I am left so choked by fear that I can hardly breathe, or so paralysed by it that I can barely move at all, let alone run? What are we to make of this disabling level of fear?

Fear according to Pi

Yann Martel, in his wonderful novel *Life of Pi*, devotes a whole, short chapter to the experience of fear. You may know the book, or have seen the film, and will recall that the protagonist finds himself at sea on a lifeboat and discovers, to his horror, that he is sharing the small rescue vessel with a fully grown tiger. His description of fear is the best I have ever encountered. Here, he describes its physical effects:

> Fear next turns fully to your body, which is already aware that something terribly wrong is going on. Already your lungs have flown away like a bird and your guts have slithered away like a snake. Now your tongue drops dead like an opossum, while your jaw begins to gallop on the spot. Your ears go deaf. Your muscles begin to shiver as if they had malaria and your knees to shake as though they were dancing. Your heart strains too hard, while your sphincter relaxes too much. And so with the rest of your body. Every part of you, in the manner most suited, falls apart. Only your eyes work well. They always pay proper attention to fear.[1]

Martel's description of fear is hardly something that equipped Pi well to deal with his dangerous fellow passenger, and yet it is an account that many of us can relate to; this is exactly what a panic attack feels like. So why does our body do this to us? For years, I assumed that panic was simply an unfortunate by-product of the need for adrenaline: a system gone wrong, overloaded in a way nature can tolerate, but never intended. And yet the more I think about anxiety and try to understand it, the more it is clear to me that even panic attacks have a purpose, because fear *must* be able to get to a point where we can no longer override it, where we are truly paralysed so that we physically *cannot* take another step towards whatever perilous situation we find ourselves in.

For panic attacks to be truly effective, they have to be both physically powerful and emotionally unpleasant; our body doesn't want to be in a perilous situation too often, so the unpleasant emotions we experience discourage us from getting into the same situation again. This explains the 'impending sense of doom' many people describe when they feel panicked; if our bodies are designed to make panic so abhorrent that we feel the world is going to end, we will make sure never to place ourselves in the same danger again.

Panic attacks, therefore, are like a smoke alarm. They are designed to wake us up when there is a major fire, and also to warn us whenever a fire might be about to happen. And so when panic attacks become a problem, we can imagine them being like a smoke alarm with a malfunction, a hair trigger that goes off with the faintest hint of fire or smoke, so much so that we can no longer even cook the dinner without it deafening us with its piercing call!

Anxiety is like pain

If you have been affected by panic attacks and wondered why on earth this is happening to you, it may help to remember that this is nature's brake; it's a way of stopping you from doing something reckless and is designed to keep you safe. The problem, as we shall see later, is when panic is triggered in response to something that is not reckless at all. This is when fear deserts us as a protective friend and becomes our gaoler.

Anxiety is a bit like pain in this regard. Pain is there to protect us from injury; medical conditions that damage the nerves that produce pain (like leprosy or diabetes, for instance) can lead to tremendous problems with tissue damage as wounds go unnoticed and infection sets in without the warning sign of pain indicating that something is wrong. Pain, like anxiety, needs to be on a sliding scale, with mild pain being an early warning sign, but something we can choose to ignore or push through to reach a higher goal – ask any keen cyclist about pushing through the pain for more on that! And yet it has to have an extreme end too – a level of pain that is physically and emotionally so unpleasant that we have to recoil, that stops us from putting our weight on a broken leg or instinctively pulls our hand away from the fire.

Pain, though, like anxiety, can become a problem. Intractable, chronic pain can be debilitating, and when you can't remove yourself from the cause of the pain or treat the underlying painful condition that led you to the doctor, chronic pain can be very difficult to live with indeed. And so too with anxiety; that useful ally that helped us to worry enough to get our essay in on time, kept us sharp and focused during a music performance or helped us worry enough about our finances that we didn't get into debt becomes a debilitating drain that grips us tightly around the chest every morning and prevents us from functioning. Or maybe it only rears its head at certain times – when we want to go on a train, or need a vaccine, or when there is a spider in the house – but when it makes its presence known, it has total control over us.

It is by understanding the true purpose of anxiety when it

works for us that we might be able to get it back in line when it acts against us. In order to understand why it might start to get out of line in the first place, we have to consider something called conditioning, often referred to as triggering, which is the subject of the next chapter.

Chapter 2

Triggers are not good or bad

They are the shortcuts to your emotions

Caught in the rain

It was the speed of my reaction that took me by surprise. How long does it take to open a door? I had no time to put my foot in the gap before I was catapulted back 40 years, my senses overwhelmed by such a keen awareness of time and place.

I was a child again on the campsite we grew up on, where we spent every summer living in a caravan and sleeping under canvas, keeping the holidaymakers happy, making sure they had paid for their pitch, selling them milk and bread in the mornings. It was the combination of sensations that took me back: the fact that I was wearing my dressing gown as I went to put out the rubbish before going to bed, the darkness of a late summer evening, the unexpected sound of heavy rain as I opened the front door.

Darkness, dressing gown, the sound and smell of rain. There were so many nights as a child when I had to wrap up warm and leave the dry comfort of my tent in the middle of the night to venture out in the rain on my way to the toilet block. It was never so bad, but rain always sounds heaviest when it falls on canvas, and darkness is deep and thick in the countryside.

They were happy years, and the campsite brings back happy memories, so, startled as I was by the sudden explosion of images and feelings that flooded my adult mind as I was stopped in my tracks on the doorstep, there was nothing unpleasant about this experience. One thing became very clear to me, however; had my childhood experience been very different, had I been assaulted on one of my night-time excursions, had fear and terror been associated with the combination of darkness, rain and dressing gown, then I would have been having a full-blown panic attack at that very moment. And the panic would have been upon me far quicker than I could think; my heart would have been leaping out of my chest and my brain would have had a lot of catching up to do.

This briefest of experiences will be something we will all be able to relate to; we have all had a time when a vivid memory or emotion is suddenly and unexpectedly brought to the forefront of our mind. Maybe it was a unique cooking smell that took us back to our grandmother's kitchen, or the taste of aniseed that recalls the sight and smell of an uncle who always had a bag of aniseed balls in his pocket. Perhaps the opening bars of a song bring with it a flood of memories, be they happy or sad. These are all examples of conditioning, a powerful and vital way that our brain learns to respond as we interact with our world.

In recent years, these powerful conditioned responses are often referred to as triggers or being triggered. There is nothing wrong with these terms, but I do have concerns that they are almost always described in a negative context, often in association with past trauma. That is understandable, since it is these negative triggers that are so unpleasant, often resulting in severe anxiety and panic. However, by only thinking of them in this negative light, we can lose sight of just how normal triggered, or conditioned, responses are, how we all have them and how they have an important role in helping us navigate the world around us. If you have triggers, please be encouraged: you are perfectly normal! I also worry about the way a word like 'trigger' can leave us feeling; some of its associations are with guns and explosions, or a trapdoor that might be triggered, emphasizing that something terrible could happen at any moment. In a way, this is accurate, because that is exactly what we feel when we are feeling anxious, but do we need a word that emphasizes this feeling when it is present already? For these reasons, I will use the more neutral word 'conditioning' in the rest of this chapter.

It's worth a detour here to explain a bit of the theory behind conditioning before we get back to what really matters, which is what it means to us in real life. Let's have a look at three concepts from the world of psychology: unconditioned responses, classical conditioning and operant conditioning.

Unconditioned responses

Conditioning is all about how we learn to respond to our environment, but not all of our responses are learned, since much of our conditioning is hardwired into our biology. These unlearned, instinctive responses are called unconditioned responses. The most obvious example would be how we instantly recoil from something painful, since our bodies contain a multitude of highly specific pain receptors, designed to respond as quickly as possible to a potential threat or injury and so keep us safe. Other unconditioned responses include the production of saliva and flow of gastric juices when we start to eat, or even with the sight or smell of food; shivering when we are cold and sweating when we are hot. Then there are more subtle responses such as how we find certain smells to be either pleasant or noxious, or the instinct to respond to a smile with a smile, present in babies when they are only eight weeks old. Some of these responses can be changed by experience – a baby deprived of human stimulation can lose the smile response, for instance – and we can even train ourselves to ignore pain if we try hard enough. Moreover, there will be genetic variation in our hardwiring; some people will not find an unpleasant smell to be noxious since they lack the gene to smell it at all, and we know that the ability to read facial expressions varies greatly, and can be hardwired – for instance, some autistic people find this particularly difficult. What characterizes unconditioned responses, however, is that there is a natural connection between the stimulus (e.g. the smell of good food) and the reaction (in this case, the production of saliva) and that while they can be influenced by learning, they do not have to be learned.

Conditioned responses

By contrast, conditioned responses occur when an association develops between a stimulus and a response that is not innate and has been learned, often in a way that is highly specific to that individual. There are two types of conditioned response, classical conditioning and operant conditioning.

Classical conditioning

You cannot talk about classical conditioning without mentioning Ivan Pavlov, the 19th-century Russian physiologist and Nobel laureate famous for his experiments with bells and dogs. Pavlov knew that dogs would salivate at the sight and smell of food, and he wondered if he could 'condition' them to salivate with a different stimulus that had nothing to do with eating. To test this theory, he created an association between food and the ringing of a bell, by ringing the bell just before food was offered to the dogs. After a while, the association between the bell and eating became so strong that the dogs would salivate just at the sound of the bell, whether food was offered or not. This is compelling science, since the production of saliva is an entirely unconscious reflex; it was the dog's primitive instincts that were learning something new here.

What is central to classical conditioning is that the response is involuntary. The dogs didn't make a conscious choice to salivate, but unconscious pathways developed this response. The behaviour of human beings is obviously more complex than that of dogs, but, as my story about rain and darkness shows, we also have primitive neurological processes that can become conditioned in a similar way. The thoughts, feelings and emotions that came back to me in a flash were not ones I had any choice over in that moment; they just happened because of my prior conditioning.

Operant conditioning

Since human learning and behaviour is complex stuff, we should hardly be surprised that classical conditioning is only one of the ways that we can learn and become conditioned. Operant conditioning is where we have developed a learned behaviour that can become deeply entrenched, but over which we have voluntary control. One key part of learning is that our actions often have consequences, and these consequences can either reinforce or diminish the emotional response we exhibit the next time we are faced with the same situation.

The seminal work on operant conditioning was performed in the 1930s by B.F. Skinner, who conducted many of the classic psychology experiments of the period. He studied the behaviour of rats as they scurried through mazes, watching how, through trial and error, they learned the quickest routes to take and which levers to press in order to receive a reward. It is easy to see how a similar learned behaviour works in humans. If, for example, every time a child tries to help in the kitchen their dad thanks them for helping and makes them feel good, they will be more likely to want to help next time. Positive emotions about cooking will be reinforced, resulting in more time spent in the kitchen. If, on the other hand, their dad were to constantly criticize them for doing it wrong and repeatedly tell them how clumsy they were, then negative emotions and feelings would be reinforced instead, and they would be more likely to avoid the kitchen when their dad is cooking.

Conditioning as a shortcut

What is key to understanding the role of conditioning in our lives is that it is neither inherently good nor bad, but it is ubiquitous and works as a convenient and important shortcut, so that we don't have to learn something from scratch every time we are faced with a stimulus. For instance, a baby will learn the smell of its mother. This is not hardwired from birth, since every person has a different smell. The baby learns to associate the smell of their unique mother and, hopefully, will associate the smell with warmth, comfort and security. Very quickly, just the smell of its mother will help to soothe the baby; it won't have to consciously think about what the smell means or why it makes everything feel okay; these emotions will just come with the smell. We see this same pattern as adults: a certain brand of perfume will instantly remind us of a particular person, or the smell of polished leather might take us back to our grandfather's workshop.

All manner of sensory stimuli will be associated with learned experience in this way. Whether it is something we see, hear, smell, taste or touch, there will be a library of associated emotions for our unconscious mind to tap into: good/bad, safe/unsafe, frightening/exciting and so on. These emotions are tapped into at speed, often below our conscious thinking, to give us a starting point in case we need to react in a hurry, and it often feels like our conscious thought has to catch up with what our body is doing. The speed with which we experience this response is important, since at times it may save our life. This is most obvious with unconditioned responses, like the stimulus to recoil from something painful, since such a response has to be as quick as possible in order to minimize injury. If we waited for our thinking brain to catch up each time before we jumped away from an unexpected painful stimulus, then we would be in a great deal of trouble!

Conditioned responses use many of the same pathways as unconditioned ones, and so often operate at the same speed – as I discovered when I opened the door to put the rubbish out. It may not be as obvious why our conditioned responses need to be so quick in our everyday lives, but it seems to me that these emotional shortcuts probably play an important role in the fluency of our lives, so that we are not constantly having to work from first principles all the time and can instead trust our instincts. I suspect that these unconscious conditioned responses allow us to have much of our operating functions on 'autopilot' most of the time so that we can focus on what we really want to be thinking about. What is more, it's not hard to think of a circumstance where a conditioned response could be lifesaving. For instance, someone with a severe peanut allergy might well become conditioned to feel revulsion at the smell of peanuts due to bad past experiences of exposure to peanuts. In these circumstances, a powerful, rapid response to the smell of peanuts might just stop them from inadvertently taking that bite of chicken kebab coated in satay sauce, and their life could be saved by this primitive reflex. When it comes to stopping us from dying, on the whole, our bodies would rather give us a hundred false alarms if it means keeping us safe from the very occasional threat. However, when it comes to anxiety, it is these false alarms that we need to look at, since they can have such an impact on our lives.

Conditioning as a cage

Billy's story is a good example of how one upsetting event led to a conditioned response that became life-controlling. Let's hear her account of how it started.

Billy's story – how it started

Until about ten years ago, I had always enjoyed flying as an exciting adventure. However, on one occasion when flying on my own, I decided to eat a burger before I boarded the plane. When it was time to board, and as I started to walk through the tunnel to the plane, I began to feel shaky and nauseous. Within minutes of taking off, I rushed to the toilet where I spent much of the journey with diarrhoea and vomiting, sweating profusely, breathing heavily, and with pins and needles in my hands and feet. I felt desperate to get off the plane, for fresh air, space, a loved one. I felt like I was dying, and this continued until at last we landed and I could get off the plane.

For the next 18 months, I would regularly experience panic attacks, predominantly brought on by claustrophobia: any enclosed space with a lack of air, being in close proximity to people, in hotel rooms with small windows, using lifts, travelling alone, cars and trains. So I would avoid this as much as possible and would carry a brown paper bag with me to help my breathing. The anxiety leading up to any new event was immense, requiring me to work through every eventuality. My prayers were often 'help me' during this time, as I had little control over my emotions.

Although a dodgy burger may well have been the cause of Billy's problems, what she is describing is a panic attack, and in this case, she became conditioned to experience the same feelings whenever she was faced with something similar, bringing back the memory of that first panic attack. While conditioning is important for keeping us from harm and can help us to think and operate fluently, tapping into deeply hidden memories in a useful way, there is no doubt that conditioning can also be highly problematic. As with Billy's story, when the emotions that are associated with a stimulus have been very frightening, we can find that these emotions become extremely debilitating whenever we are exposed to the same situation in the future, because panic sets in.

A story of panic attacks like the one Billy experienced can build up slowly over time but, as in Billy's case, there is often an initial frightening or traumatic event where it all started. When I see patients with panic attacks, they occasionally come to me with the first panic attack and we can talk through what has happened; more often, though, the events are rare enough that the panic attacks have become normalized: 'I just can't do planes,' we tell ourselves, in the same matter-of-fact way that we might say, 'I have red hair,' or 'I don't like rice pudding.' Since avoiding flying is an easy thing to do (more on the role of avoidance in anxiety will be discussed in Chapter 4), these panic attacks can be kept relatively infrequent, until they start to leak out into other situations, like not going on trains or taking long car journeys.

At this point, someone may come to see me, because it has become a problem and they don't know what to do. When this happens, I find that a useful question to ask relates to the very first time my patient had a panic attack. Questions like 'What happened that time? Tell me all about it,' 'What happened before you felt panicky?' and 'What happened next?' will often reveal how the conditioning started: how this person who used to enjoy travelling had their first panic attack. Once we have found out what made the association, then we can start to talk about how we unravel it.

Deconditioning

The most important thing to know about conditioning is that it is not fixed and, just as it can be learned, it can also be unlearned – something known as deconditioning. This is sometimes called extinction learning or extinction conditioning, which may be a useful term if we want to consider ourselves to be making our fear extinct, although it is a bit too alarming a word for me to be comfortable using in the context of talking about anxiety!

Deconditioning involves the gradual fading of the link between the stimulus and the conditioned response. This was demonstrated by Pavlov in his experiments with dogs. Once he had conditioned the dogs to salivate at the sound of a bell, he continued his experiments with these same dogs, exposing them to both the bell and food, but now at different times so that there was no association between the two. Gradually, over time, the dogs stopped producing saliva at the sound of the bell. What is important about deconditioning is that while conditioning can develop gradually or be triggered by a single dramatic event, deconditioning is usually gradual as the association fades.

In practice, this means that the way to reduce the power of panic is to gradually expose yourself to the situation that makes you panic – a scary thought that we will consider in more detail in Chapter 12. For the moment, let's just leave it here that the association can diminish and can even be broken entirely, so that panic recedes into the background and even disappears for good. Let's return to Billy's story and see how things worked out for her.

Billy's story – realization and recovery

After the 18-month period, I tried to work out what was happening to me. I knew I wasn't afraid of dying, so why was I now living in this place of fear and anxiety?

I was perfectly well physically and emotionally before I ate the burger, so it was clear to see that the burger had upset me – maybe it was food poisoning? In normal circumstances, I would have been able to access a comfortable place to be unwell, with family support and reassurance. This helped me understand the process of events that took place on the plane. The start of the nausea caused the claustrophobia, and the exhaustion of being sick led to a panic attack and the fear of death.

I was able to rationalize effectively from now on. Every time I felt anxious, I would tell myself that I ate a burger which upset me and caused a panic attack; I was not afraid of dying. Rather than continue to avoid fearful situations, I developed tools to manage my anxiety when it came and started to face these situations once more. I began to travel further distances in the car and on the train alone. I stayed away for weekends with friends, and, two years on, I eventually travelled on a plane with my family. Although periodically the unhealthy learned behaviours like to remind me of their presence, I choose to ignore them and not allow them to take control of me.

This took at least five years to fully overcome, and since then I have travelled on a plane alone!

Billy's story is not uncommon, and it gives us hope to see that once she properly understood what had happened to her, she could start to turn things around. It is that understanding, or the nature of anxiety and how it is never foolish or ridiculous, that we will look at in the next chapter.

Chapter 3

Anxiety is never foolish or ridiculous

It just sometimes feels that way

We have seen that anxiety is an important protective mechanism, there to stop us from getting into trouble, and how conditioning helps our body to know what to fear and what not to, so that we can react quickly when we need to. But one of the most puzzling things about anxiety is how we can become anxious about seemingly the silliest things that couldn't possibly harm us.

Phobias are the most obvious example of this. Let's take the most classic phobia of all as an example: arachnophobia, the fear of spiders. Living in the UK, there is no logical reason to be afraid of spiders. Although some of them are highly venomous, their mouthparts are too small to penetrate human skin and so they are no risk to us at all. The false widow spider is one of the few that can give an unpleasant bite, but even this spider is in no way dangerous. So why do so many people have such a strong reaction to spiders when they see one?

There are many reasons why spiders might generate fear. After all, in some parts of the world, spider bites can be highly dangerous and even fatal. In Australia, home to some 4000 different species of spider, including many that are truly dangerous, it may pay to be arachnophobic. Perhaps we have evolved to be fearful of spiders? It would make sense that we might have some in-built aversion to something that could be harmful; this is what the psychoanalyst Carl Jung described as the 'collective unconscious' and might include a fearful bias against spiders. Interestingly, though, the incidence of this phobia among Australians, where such evolutionary pressure would make the most sense, is similar to the rest of the world – around 5 per cent of the population. And most people don't mind spiders at all; some even love them! This is not something like a raging fire or an earthquake that would cause us all to be terrified, so any genetic predisposition towards a fear of spiders cannot be that strong.

Even if there is some unconscious benefit to being afraid of spiders, how does that explain some of the more unusual phobias, such as a fear of cotton wool, or buttons, or bananas? All of these genuinely exist, and although they are less common, those affected have exactly the same disabling feelings of panic when confronted with their specific fear as someone afraid of spiders will experience, or as I did when I was terrified of dogs as a child.

Cynophobia – my story

Cynophobia is the name given to an extreme fear of dogs. I can't remember a time in my childhood when I wasn't afraid of dogs, but at the time I certainly didn't think my reaction was in any way extreme – dogs were terrifying!

My fear was epitomized by what I believed to be the most terrifying dog of them all, the Alsatian or German Shepherd. Alsatians were, in my mind, bred to be vicious – they were used as police dogs and guard dogs after all! I had reason to be afraid! Even seeing a *Beware of the Dog* sign would always bring to my mind the image of a salivating Alsatian and raise the hairs on the back of my neck.

And yet my fear went far beyond what was a logical reaction to a dog that could genuinely harm me. There was many a time when my older sister, who loved dogs, was deprived of any chance of saying hello to them because I made such a fuss until our parents removed us from the vicinity of a dog, no matter whether the dog was big or small, fierce or cute. There was the occasion when our infant schoolteacher took my mum aside to ask why my sister and I kept being late for school; it turned out that I always insisted we walked the long way to school to avoid passing the house with the dog. (I still can't quite believe that we walked on our own to infant school, but that's a different matter!) And there was the paper round that I gave up because of the stress of delivering papers to houses where dogs barked.

My fear was on a spectrum from what seemed a highly rational reaction to large dogs that certainly do need to be treated with respect, to the highly irrational reaction to dogs that were never going to harm me. What I can remember most from that time was not the dogs themselves, but the dry mouth, rapid heart-beat and sweaty palms that came whenever a dog of any sort was nearby.

The dictionary definition of a phobia is 'an extreme or irrational fear of or aversion to something'.

The word 'irrational' is written into the very way we define phobias, and is how many people feel about their phobias, but is it justified, and is it fair to those affected to label them as being irrational? Chris Hall is a columnist for *The Guardian* newspaper and wrote a very frank article in 2019 where he described his fear of cotton wool:

> My family refer to cotton wool as CW when I'm around. It's their little way of acknowledging my odd phobia and that I don't even like hearing the words cotton wool, let alone coming into contact with the stuff. My heart races, saliva rushes into my mouth, the hairs on my arms and neck stand up, I get goose bumps, my toes curl, my hands become fists. I feel sick at the thought of the very particular way in which it would feel and squeak between my fingers. I've learned not to scream in horror, but inside I'm churning.[2]

Cotton wool can't be dangerous, surely? It must be irrational to be afraid of cotton wool! But that is the wrong way to approach what is happening here. The question we must ask ourselves is this: if cotton wool made you feel like that, would it not be entirely rational to be afraid of it? Panic attacks are frightening and horrible to experience, so if something seemingly harmless is going to trigger a panic attack in you, then it takes on a new danger for you. It becomes harmful to you, not because it is inherently dangerous, but because it will trigger a panic attack, which will have seriously unpleasant physical and psychological effects on your wellbeing. It has become harmful, and so it is *entirely rational* to fear it. We have become anxious not so much about the object of our fear, but about the fear we are going to feel if we have any association with it – we have become afraid of fear itself.

This explains why even the thought of cotton wool, even its very name, triggered the feelings of panic for Chris, because when we have become conditioned to be afraid of something, then that fear can be triggered in all manner of ways. These triggers will especially act through our senses – what we can see, hear, feel, smell, touch and taste – but even thoughts themselves can activate the pathway to anxiety and panic. Of course, there will be a sliding scale in the intensity of reaction we are subject to, which Chris describes in his article, but even at the 'mildest' end of the scale, the reaction was sufficient to render the words 'cotton wool' off limits to his family when Chris was within earshot.

Although phobias are the most obvious example of something triggering anxiety, the same rational explanation can be given for other types of anxiety. Take social anxiety, for instance. If going out and seeing people makes you feel stressed and anxious, does it not make sense to be anxious about going out and seeing people? Others might try to reassure you that it will be fine, that the people you are seeing are your friends and want you to be there and that everyone will be nice to you. But this all becomes irrelevant when you know it will trigger fear. Going out for the evening isn't about having fun anymore; it's about living with fear.

Or take health anxiety. If feeling symptoms in your chest triggers you to panic that something is seriously wrong with your heart, isn't it logical to become fearful of symptoms in your chest? Your doctor might reassure you that nothing is wrong and there is nothing to be afraid of – which might help for a while – but when you next get a pain there, it will trigger the same anxiety and make you feel afraid. Health anxiety is such a unique challenge, because of the interplay between our emotions and our physical symptoms, that it has earned itself its own chapter in this book, so we will cover this fully in Chapter 7.

Whatever the unique circumstances behind each person's fear, we need a new language to describe the cause of fear and to change the implication that it is irrational. The terms we use to describe medical problems have usually been created by well-meaning doctors but without reference to the people who are actually affected by the condition. It would be fascinating to form a focus group of people who live with phobias to discuss the dictionary definition of their fear as being irrational – I suspect that the conclusion of the group would be that it is neither true nor helpful.

Generalized anxiety disorder – more of the same

Doctors use the term generalized anxiety disorder (GAD) when someone feels anxious in a wide range of situations, rather than something specific like with a phobia or social anxiety, but it is really more of the same. Rather than a simple, direct link between one stimulus and anxiety, the conditioned response is more like a network of learned associations and behaviours, leading to a habitual tendency to worry and feel anxious. It may be worsened by certain situations, such as going out, socializing or being put in the spotlight, but the anxiety is usually there in the background. Sometimes there is no obvious reason why someone is affected by anxiety in this way; sometimes genetics play a part and sometimes this generalized form of anxiety relates to past traumas and struggles. While it may be important to unpick some of the underlying causes of GAD with a therapist, the understanding of anxiety in the here and now is exactly the same – when situations make you anxious, it is natural and logical to fear them, whatever they are.

Panic as a false alarm

Once we have understood that it makes perfect, rational sense to be afraid of seemingly trivial things, we can also start to understand how the panic that results is a false alarm. It is a failure of conditioning where the big red panic button in our psyche is triggered by something we would not normally be afraid of. It seems to be a quirk of evolution, where it is so important to trigger the alarm when something genuinely threatening comes along that a few false alarms along the way are a small price to pay. The problem is that in our modern world there are so many stimuli to respond to that these false alarms pop up all the time. In times gone by, there would have been no risk of developing a false alarm to cotton wool, or injections, or flying, or the telephone, since these are all modern inventions. We should not be surprised that false alarms of panic pop up. Once we have established them as false alarms, we can learn how to disconnect the alarm system. First, however, we need to look at what we usually do, which is exactly the opposite. This is such a big issue that it is the subject of the next three chapters.

Chapter 4

Avoidance makes sense

Why would you do something that makes you scared?

I'm not a big fan of walking on Lego bricks. I did it a few times when my children were younger, and I'm always left with the same cluster of thoughts racing round my head as I hop around on one foot, clutching its injured partner and trying not to swear. 'How can something so small cause so much pain?', 'How can I have trodden on Lego *again*?' and 'Who left that on the floor?!' are three that immediately spring to mind.

And so, back in the day, when Lego was a regular feature on our living-room floor, I did my best to avoid treading on Lego bricks. It made sense: standing on the bricks causes me pain; it is something I *can* avoid and so I wanted to avoid it happening again. I did my best to make sure the Lego was all tidied away after the fun was over, I encouraged my children to do the same and I kept a lookout for stray bricks when my feet were bare. My mother went one step further when I was a child and threatened to fine us 10p for every brick she found after we claimed to have put them all away!

Avoiding things that are painful makes perfect sense. Since anxiety is a bit like pain, and can be just as unpleasant, if not more so, it also makes perfect sense to avoid something if it makes us anxious. We don't even need to think it through; all our instincts tell us to do it and the powerful shortcut mechanism of conditioning has the express purpose of helping us to avoid things quickly, so that we can escape from danger. The instinct to run happens well before we have time to think about it properly.

Much of the time, avoidance is also a perfectly helpful and important strategy. I have successfully avoided walking along the middle of a motorway for my entire life; indeed, the very thought of it makes me anxious, and avoiding doing this has kept me safe and served me well. More importantly, this avoidance strategy for walking on motorways has not curtailed my life in any way. However, what if it were not *walking* on motorways that I was avoiding, but *driving* on them? Just as in my slightly silly example, I will have avoided the anxiety associated with being on the motorway, as well as avoiding the undeniable risk of having an accident on a motorway, but the crucial difference is that now my life has been constrained.

It might not be a big thing – it depends on how much I might like or need to travel, and how important motorways could be on the journeys I would like to take, but certainly there could be some inconvenience in not being able to drive on a motorway. Maybe I only have to avoid it if I am the driver (or maybe I can only do it if I *am* the driver!); either way, it is still bringing some restriction on my freedom to travel.

The fact is, though, that if I am fearful of driving on motorways, then the only way to completely avoid having to feel that fear is to avoid driving on the motorway – and so it makes perfect sense that this is the most likely action I will take. It might make my journey longer as I travel down smaller roads to get to my destination. It might actually *increase* my risk of having an accident, since accidents are far more likely to happen on smaller roads than on a motorway, but it is not the risk of an accident I am trying to avoid; it is the fear I feel when I think about the motorway.

What is more, there is a fine line between avoiding something because it makes us anxious and avoiding it because we just aren't that keen on it anyway. I avoid playing golf mostly because I don't find it that interesting (sorry, golfers!). In truth, I am not often asked to play, but even if I were invited, I know I would turn down the offer. Is it just because I find it a bit dull? Well, mostly, but I know I would find it a bit stressful too. I would be entering a new world with its own language, rules and conventions. Would I annoy the people coming behind me because I was playing too slowly? What if I damaged the green? Would I be wearing the right clothes? There's no doubt that the stress I would feel – the anxiety it would generate – puts me off, but largely I choose not to play golf because there are always other things I would rather do with my time.

Avoiding, or just choosing not to?

Life is all about the choices we make; we can't do everything, so we choose to do some things and choose not to do others. How, then, do we know if we are choosing not to do something simply because we are not that keen on it, or perhaps because we find it inherently unpleasant, or because we are avoiding the anxiety it creates? With golf, I am sure that for me it is mostly a lack of inter-est, but there are other things I avoid where the balance is more in favour of anxiety. Take performing, for instance. I actually love some forms of performance – like giving a talk or teaching a group of people. I might be apprehensive beforehand, but it gives me a buzz to perform in this way and so I take the opportunity to do it when I can. But don't ask me to act or sing on a stage!

In many ways, my aversion to acting in particular is a bit odd

(I am not a great singer, so this is more understandable). Much of how I like to teach is very interactive and *ad lib*; often it involves role play where we work with actors playing the role of patients as a way of honing communication skills. Role play is acting, and most doctors hate it, but I genuinely enjoy it! I have given talks on a stage to large audiences, and the bigger the audience, the bigger the buzz I get from it; surely I should also love the idea of acting on a stage, and yet the very idea of it brings a sense of dread! I know I would find the whole experience very uncomfortable, and so I avoid it. There are other things I would rather be doing with my time, and so I am quite content not to tread the boards, but I know that what really stops me from taking up acting is not a lack of time or interest but the anxiety it would provoke. Why is there a difference? It is not an inherently scarier thing to do than giving a talk; I have colleagues who would dread giving a lecture and yet love a bit of amateur dramatics.

I'm sure part of it is based on past experience – I can remember the buzz from teaching that has gone well, but still recall acute embarrassment from times in my life when I have been persuaded to act. And, ultimately, I have never challenged my resistance to acting; I have always been content to opt out, and so I have never discovered if I could overcome my anxiety and learn to love it.

It is also important to realize that there are some things we avoid because, to us at least, they are inherently unpleasant. This can be true for anyone, but it is particularly important to recognize this for people who are neurodivergent. My own example of this is rollercoasters. I actually quite enjoy the thrill of a rollercoaster, and I don't feel anxious about being on one, but the nausea I feel with anything that twists and turns too much can be unbearable and can take hours to recover from. Avoiding certain rides is just a wise choice for me! For people who are neurodivergent, this can be a particularly important issue to consider, since sensory overload or the exhaustion of having to interpret the social cues of large numbers of people can make particular situations very difficult to navigate. Of course, a neurodivergent person can have anxiety as well and needs to be mindful about why they might avoid doing something, or perhaps consider changing their approach to it (such as wearing headphones to cope with loud noise, for instance), but it is important to acknowledge that avoidance needs to be considered differently in this situation.

The reinforcement of avoidance

Our choice to avoid something is rarely a one-off decision, since most of what we avoid due to anxiety are situations we are faced with time and again. This may be on a daily basis if we have something like social anxiety, or it may only happen in certain circumstances, such as a needle phobia or avoiding going into a room when we know there is a spider in there. Each time we avoid something, however, it reinforces the need to avoid it in the future and increases the chance of it extending into other areas of our lives. Let's look at an example of how this reinforcement can occur.

A series of logical jumps

THE FIRST JUMP

Surahi had never liked frogs; there was something in their unnaturally slimy skin, goggle eyes and the sudden unpredictability of how they jump that turned her stomach, set her heart racing and put the hairs on the back of her neck on edge. And so, when she met up with her friend Rebecca, Surahi always offered to host; it was better that way, what with Rebecca's pond.

THE SECOND JUMP

Sometimes they would meet in a park, but not the one with the lake. Not anymore – not after *that* incident! She hated to think about it; Rebecca said it wasn't that close, but Surahi was sure it had jumped on to her friend's foot! No, the park with the lake wasn't that nice anyway. Surahi always checked carefully before they met in a park – wasn't it helpful that Google maps always showed rivers and lakes?

THE THIRD JUMP

It was best to meet indoors really. It was just as nice with the French doors open and you didn't have to worry about sun cream. Rebecca didn't seem to mind. Surahi didn't realize just how far they would go from water – in *her* garden! There weren't even any ponds nearby as far as she knew. No, she didn't go in the garden much now, really. But then Ash had always been the gardener in the family.

THE FOURTH JUMP

Rebecca did think the board was rather odd, but she was polite about it. 'The Frog Board' the family called it – and what a good idea it was! It meant the French doors could be wide open and yet there was no need to worry about the frogs jumping in! Surahi was so glad she'd thought about it as it had been getting stifling in the lounge with the doors closed.

As for many people when they start avoiding something, Surahi's avoidance took a series of steps as it evolved over time. Often these steps happen so slowly that we don't notice them, as each step becomes normalized before we take the next one. Ironically for Surahi, we are rather like the apocryphal frog that fails to jump out of the water when the pan is slowly brought to the boil! By the time Surahi was at the stage of using 'the Frog Board', her avoidance of frogs had become rather odd and very restrictive in her life, but it had become normal to her and her family.

Confirmation bias and avoidance

Confirmation bias is something we are all prone to and it can play an important role in reinforcing our beliefs, and our fears. This type of bias is where we tend to favour new information when it confirms our previously held beliefs and are more likely to dismiss it if it is contrary to our beliefs.

A simple example of confirmation bias would be my belief that gardening is good for your mental health. I am heavily invested in this belief for several reasons: I recommend gardening to my patients, gardening is one of the main ways I like to keep myself well, and I am a trustee of a community garden for wellbeing near our GP practice. As a result, when I read a report like the King's Fund report on the health benefits of gardening, I am inclined to focus on all the good bits that show how amazing gardening can be for wellbeing. Any areas where the report says there is no evidence that gardening helps health are the bits I'm likely to skip over. If I read a paper that suggested gardening was *bad* for your health, I would probably find a good reason to dismiss it entirely. (I can hear myself now: 'Well, it might say that gardeners are more prone to having a bad back, but back pain is common, maybe they would have got it anyway? And think of the benefits, at least it gets them outdoors!')

This tendency to confirm our underlying beliefs can also reinforce our fears. If we are anxious about getting on a train, we will tend to notice *every* train crash on the news and ignore the evidence that trains are a far safer form of transport than travelling by car. It won't matter that the reason we became anxious on trains had nothing to do with crashing and everything to do with being able to access a toilet on a journey; the *feeling* of fear associated with trains will be reinforced by hearing about a crash, and that will confirm our *belief* that trains are to be avoided.

Confirmation bias not only affects how we interpret external information but is also at the root of an internal feedback loop that reinforces our instinct to avoid. The more we avoid something, the less practice we get at doing it, and so the more we believe we can't do it. Let's take an example outside of the area of mental health to illustrate this.

Ben and Jerry learn piano

Let's imagine that Ben and Jerry take a break from making ice cream (it's okay, they have plenty of stock; we won't run out!) and decide to learn piano. They start at the same level and, after a few months, neither of them is very good yet, but anyone hearing them play would say they were playing at the same level.

However, Ben lacks confidence and is highly critical of himself. As a result, he tends to feel bad and frustrated when he plays, and so avoids practising. He doesn't avoid it entirely; he is just reluctant to practise because he believes he isn't a good player. Jerry, on the other hand, also knows he isn't that great, but he keeps on practising anyway.

A year passes and, in that time, Jerry has done twice as much practice as his friend. Not surprisingly, when they sit their Grade exam Jerry passes with a merit, while Ben only gets a straight pass. Ben's false and biased belief from a year earlier that he was a less good player than his friend has now been confirmed; he genuinely is a less good player now.

Ben's experience is played out by anxious people every day; those who believe they are no good at talking to people at parties shy away from talking and so get little practice at it. The more they avoid it, the more they lose confidence in their ability to know what to say, and the more it confirms their biased belief that they are hopeless at parties. Of course, this is why it is rarely helpful to just tell someone they are good at something when they are not. It would only annoy Ben to pretend he was as good as Jerry at the piano, when their Grade exam results are incontrovertible proof that this is not the case. If someone avoids parties due to their anxiety, it's not realistic to expect them to become the life and soul of a party overnight!

Understanding that your internal bias may have led to you getting out of practice may help you to understand the processes that have led to some of the difficulties you face. More importantly, it can help you gain an understanding of why a decision to practise the very things that make you anxious can be so important, and so effective, in helping to reduce the amount that anxiety restricts your life.

Confirmation bias, therefore, is a powerful reinforcer of the beliefs and feelings that underpin our instinct to avoid. We can never eliminate confirmation bias entirely from the way we think, but being aware of it can certainly help us to limit its impact, especially if we want to work on overcoming our fears.

Avoidance as a strategy

Avoidance is therefore an instinctive, rational and entirely understandable strategy for dealing with anxiety. Moreover, on an immediate level, it is frequently successful. If you want to avoid anxiety here, today, right now, then avoidance is usually your best bet. The problem with avoidance, however, is that it is terribly short-sighted; it pays no attention to tomorrow and is deeply flawed as a long-term strategy, which is the subject of the next chapter.

Chapter 5

Avoidance binds us in soft, silken ribbons

They can be so comfortable we don't even know we're tied up

The huge problem with avoidance as a strategy for dealing with anxiety is that it is so effective! At least in the short term. In the here-and-now present moment, the most effective, most comforting strategy of all is to avoid. It reminds me of a Peanuts cartoon strip where Linus, the young boy who always carries his comfort blanket with him, is talking to Charlie Brown: 'I don't like to face problems head-on,' he declares. 'I think the best way to deal with problems is to avoid them. This is a distinct philosophy of mine: no problem is so big or so complicated that it can't be run away from!'[3] Avoidance is truly comforting, but it is like being tied up in soft, silken ribbons; we might feel comforted by their silky feel, but we are tied up, nevertheless.

Yann Martel's eloquent evocation of fear, quoted

in Chapter 1, describes when you have a full-blown panic attack and your whole body deserts you for its duration. He goes on to explain how your natural, understandable, overriding instinct will be to avoid it happening again. However, Martel also warns us of the danger of doing this:

> The matter is difficult to put into words. For fear, real fear, such as shakes you to your foundation, such as you feel when you are brought face to face with your mortal end, nestles in your memory like a gangrene: it seeks to rot everything, even the words with which to speak of it. So you must fight hard to express it. You must fight hard to shine the light of words upon it. Because if you don't, if your fear becomes a wordless darkness that you avoid, perhaps even manage to forget, you open yourself to further attacks of fear because you never fought the opponent who defeated you.[4]

What Martel is describing is the reinforcement of conditioning. When we have an episode of anxiety like this, it reinforces our negative conditioning about whatever led to us becoming afraid, so that we are even more likely to react with fear the next time we encounter the same situation – this is what he means by 'nestles in your memory like a gangrene'. We know that the way to reduce conditioning, or to decondition ourselves to use the proper term, is to experience the same situation but without the associated fear – or with the fear feeling more controlled. If we remember Pavlov's dogs from Chapter 2, every time they experienced the bell and food at the same time, it strengthened the association between food and the bell, therefore strengthening their conditioning. It was only when they heard the bell at times when there was no food that the conditioning began to reduce. So, by avoiding situations that make us anxious, we are also *avoiding our main hope of improving the situation*. The fear becomes more powerful each time we experience it, and this is sustained in the depths of our mind all the time we avoid it, only to assail us once more when the opportunity arises. Indeed, every time we avoid, we imagine the fear we might have felt had we not chosen the safe, comforting option of avoidance, and even this imagined fear strengthens the hold it has over us.

What is more, avoiding can become a habit that spreads to other areas of our lives. What started as simply avoiding the office party leads to avoiding other social events, then deciding to eat your lunch on your own, avoiding going into the town centre when it's busy, avoiding the town centre altogether and so on. There is every danger that your world becomes smaller and smaller as your anxiety creates more and more 'no-go' areas and life becomes more limited. Sometimes this happens in such gradual steps that you hardly notice, while other times a highly traumatic event, or a societal event like the COVID-19 pandemic, leads to a sea change in what you can and cannot do.

Fundamentally, avoidance is a 'here and now' strategy that is only interested in reducing the experience of anxiety in the present moment, with a flagrant disregard for our future happiness. Sometimes we need to step back and see how this is affecting us and how much of a problem avoidance has created.

What are you avoiding?

One question I often ask patients is this: 'What does your anxiety stop you from doing?' It's a really helpful question to ask yourself and it is well worth considering. I often find that patients need a moment to stop and think; usually, they do best to go away and really work through it and then come back to me. You might want to do the same and put the book down for a moment while you spend time with this. Once you have identified areas of your life that you avoid because they make you anxious, there are two more questions to ask:

1. How do other people react to the situation that makes you anxious?
2. Does it matter to you that you avoid this?

We will consider these questions in turn.

How do other people react?

This is not the most important question, since ultimately it is what matters to you that is important, not what matters to most people – but it can still be helpful to ask ourselves. The reason for this is that often our behaviour can be unusual, but we have got so used to it that we don't stop and think about it; it has become *normalized* to us. It can help to calibrate what we do in a certain situation by comparing it to what other people do. We can take this at a range of levels depending on the situation. If we consider the example of Surahi and her frog phobia from the previous chapter, for instance, we might come up with something like Table 5.1 on the opposite page.

It may be helpful to ask someone who knows you well to help you think about one of your fears in this way, since you might have justified how you react to certain situations by convincing yourself that it is not that unusual. Surahi's situation is relatively simple to analyse since it is such a specific phobia, but what about a more complex fear, such as social phobia (a fear of being in social situations where you might be subject to the scrutiny of others) or agoraphobia (a fear of being in a situation from which you might not be able to escape, which can often make it very difficult to leave the house at all)? It is still possible to look at situations that might be difficult and tabulate them.

Table 5.1: Surahi's frog phobia

Surahi's situation	How other people might react	Conclusion
Surahi is afraid of frogs.	Most people are not afraid of frogs, but some fear of frogs or an aversion to them is quite common. Surahi is not unusual in being afraid of frogs.	Surahi's aversion to frogs is not unusual.
Surahi avoids going to her friend's house because of the pond in the garden.	Most people are able to enjoy ponds and many with an aversion to frogs would be able to sit in a garden with a pond, but some would find this difficult.	Surahi's avoidance of her friend's garden is unusual, but not that uncommon.
Surahi avoids going to any park that has water near it.	Most people have no issue with going to a park with a pond, and many people with an aversion to frogs would be able to go to a park with a pond, but some would avoid it, or at least sit away from the water.	Surahi is not alone in her avoidance of parks with water, but maybe her checking on Google maps before visiting any park is unusual.
Surahi avoids going in her own garden because she encountered a frog there once.	Many people actively enjoy seeing a frog, while most people with an aversion to frogs would be unhappy about coming across a frog in the garden, but it would not stop them from going into their own garden.	Surahi is quite unusual in not being able to go into her own garden, and most people would be surprised that she could not do this, and feel it is very restrictive for her.
Surahi either keeps the French doors closed, or uses the frog board to prevent frogs from jumping into the house.	Most people, even those with an aversion to frogs, would think this was very unusual behaviour and would never even think that a frog might jump into a house.	This is highly unusual behaviour.

It might help to put them in order, with either the most difficult or the least difficult at the top. In Table 5.2, I have considered what you might put for social anxiety. Here I have put harder things at the top. I have just imagined situations that you might find difficult, but I could be way off the mark, so it is important to put your own situations down and put them in the order that is right for you. Also, put them in the order in which your *anxiety* makes it difficult, rather than any other reason. You might dislike family gatherings, for instance, but it's whether or not they make you anxious that matters here, not how you feel about that annoying relative who's always there!

When you complete the last column in the table, you may also want to consider what most people *like you* would do. For instance, if you are a professional musician and have started to become anxious about performing, you may want to compare your reaction to that of other professional musicians, since non-musicians would never consider performing in an orchestra in the first place. Or if you are neurodivergent, how do other neurodivergent people react? Some neurodivergent people are particularly affected by sensory overload, for instance, an area that may not be an issue at all to neurotypical people. If this is you, then you would do well to compare with other neurodivergent people – do they all react like you do? How do other neurodivergent people manage situations with sensory overload? Does your reaction cause a problem?

Does it matter to you?

Giving time to think about how avoidance has affected you will help you to understand the challenges you face. You may have gone through this exercise and decided that there is not too much to worry about; you do get anxious at times, but it is not restricting you to any great extent, in which case you may not need to make any changes at all.

Table 5.2: Social phobia

Social situation	What you do	What most people would do
Acting/dancing/ singing on a stage		
Going to a party where you don't know many people		
Going to a party where you know most people		
Going to see a small group of friends		
Going shopping when the shops are busy		
Going shopping when the shops are quiet		
Going to a family gathering		
Going for a walk with a friend		
Going to work/ school/college		
Leaving the house on your own		
Leaving the house with someone else		

However, as you have chosen to read this book, there is a chance that you (or someone you want to support) are feeling overwhelmed right now, that you feel the challenges are insurmountable and you don't know where to start with overcoming them. If that is you, then don't lose heart! With the right understanding of what you are facing, and the right sort of help, it is possible to make tremendous progress with anxiety. There is a world of difference between feeling that anxiety is in control of you and feeling that you are in control of it, and so the first goal is to regain a sense of control. That really is something you can achieve, although it might involve hard work!

The fact that regaining control over anxiety does involve work, and hard work at times, means it is really important to consider the second question: does it matter to you? Because it is only if it matters to you that you should think about doing something about it, and it is only if it *really matters* to you that you will be willing to put in the hard work to make progress. It is a bit like being able to run 5K. The well-known 'Couch to 5K' app can help you get to the 5K distance, but running is hard work, so you have to actually *want* to be able to run that far before you will put the effort into using the app. In the same way, much of the rest of this book will be focused on the tools that can help you push back against anxiety; tools like understanding how your thoughts, feelings and actions interact, and the principles of cognitive behavioural therapy. It isn't all hard work – some of it will be about learning to rest properly, how to avoid bad habits and get better sleep, and I will also discuss the role of medication – but there will be effort required as well. You are like an athlete in training or a military veteran recovering from injury; you need rehabilitation, and you need to decide which parts of your life you want to rehabilitate.

For instance, you may avoid thrill-seeking behaviour, like rollercoaster rides, because it makes you anxious; other people may think you are missing out on all the fun, but, in reality, you are living a very fulfilled life without these activities, so why spend effort trying to overcome your anxiety here? Or you may have a minor phobia about spiders: you really prefer someone else to deal with one when they show themselves, but you can handle them if you have to and have developed a nifty strategy with a cordless vacuum cleaner that serves you very well. Or maybe it is a bigger problem and means you can't sleep in a room on your own for fear of the spiders that might be under the bed, and this is becoming a major inconvenience. Perhaps you have a needle phobia, and now that you have developed a medical condition that involves regular blood tests, it is starting to cause you difficulties, or your social phobia is making it difficult to go to work and you keep making excuses when your friends invite you out.

So, does it matter to you? Are you annoyed enough about your anxiety affecting you in this way that you are ready to do something about it? Don't think for the moment about what to do, or if it will work, or if you can actually do it – take it on faith for now that something can be done to improve things, and decide if you are ready for change.

You may find it helpful to think of the stages of change here.

The stages of change

The stages of change were first described by Prochaska and Di-Clemente about 40 years ago[5] and it can be really helpful to think about where you are in this cycle:

1. Precontemplative: you haven't even been thinking about change.
2. Contemplative: you are thinking about change but haven't decided if you want to do it yet, or made any plans.

3. Preparation: you have decided to change and are trying to work out how to do it.
4. Action: you have put plans into place and made a change.
5. Maintenance: the change is in place, and it is now a question of keeping it there.
6. Relapse: it is never inevitable that relapse occurs, but we always have to be realistic that this is a normal part of the stages of change, and many changes go through multiple, full or partial relapses before they are maintained.

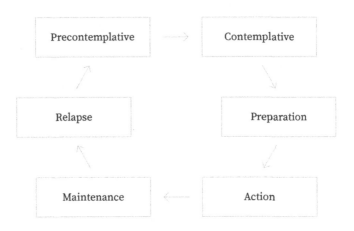

The model was developed with a view to helping people make changes like stopping smoking, reducing alcohol intake or exercising more, but it can be just as useful with any change we might want to make in our lives, especially when that change is challenging. The decision to change a long-held strategy of avoidance is no small thing, and many people spend years in the precontemplative stage, not even thinking that they could change.

When I read about Chris Hall's fear of cotton wool that I referred to in Chapter 3, I was struck by the tragedy that he had got to the age of 48 before he considered change. Before that, he had always found ways to work around it; probably he hadn't even realized that it could be treated – it was just who he was and how things were. It was the coming of children, first with the need to use cotton wool when changing nappies and then with the realization that he did not want to pass his fear on to his children, that finally moved him from precontemplative to contemplative, and then quite quickly into preparation and action as he sought therapy. And already he has seen progress and can shout out the words 'cotton wool' from the rooftops without fear setting in!

The cycle of change is also very important if you are helping someone else tackle their anxiety. You may want them to change and, in your desperation for them to make progress, it is very easy to rush ahead of them in the cycle: they are still precontemplative while you are on the phone trying to book them into therapy. Arranging therapy is an action stage, so you are two steps further round the cycle than they are, which rarely ends well. The most likely outcome is that they will harden their resistance and you will become frustrated. If you are helping anyone with change, try to nudge them gently around the cycle of change by all means, but take it one step at a time and don't rush ahead!

On my Instagram page, there is one video where I make custard! Odd as it sounds, it might help here. When you mix the right amount of custard powder with water it makes a wonderful substance known as oobleck, which is named after a Dr Seuss book, *Bartholomew and the Oobleck*. It is what is known as a non-Newtonian fluid. Newtonian fluids only change their viscosity when you change their temperature – so oil, for instance, becomes runnier when you heat it up and thicker when you cool it down. Non-Newtonian fluids, however, change their viscosity when other forces are applied to them. Oobleck has the remarkable feature that it massively increases its viscosity, becoming a putty-like solid, when you apply pressure, and rapidly becomes liquid again once the pressure is removed. I often illustrate this when I teach GP trainees about the GP consultation, since it allows for a fun demonstration where I make up the oobleck in a mixing bowl and then ask an unsuspecting trainee to don an apron and punch the mixture! They are usually game for a laugh and are greatly relieved when their fist lands softly in the putty rather than hitting the bottom of the glass bowl. It has a serious point, though; people can be like oobleck – if we meet resistance to change, then the more we push, the more they will harden their resistance, yet if we stop pushing and start listening, they will soften. So, if someone you care about is resistant to change, think of custard and don't push too hard!

Avoidance is a many-headed beast

There are many things that can help your anxiety, but a fundamental key to unlocking progress is to change the flawed strategy of avoidance – to start untying its ribbons and set ourselves free. Avoidance is the cardinal sign of anxiety; it is its calling card, its shadow. What is more, it is also a many-headed beast; if we are going to show it the door, then we need to understand it in all its guises, else it will appear to go humbly out the front door and sneak round the back and into our lives once more, tricking us into believing it has gone when it has just changed form. This multiplicity of avoidance, therefore, will be the subject of the next chapter.

Chapter 6

Avoidance is sneaky

Don't let it get away with it!

The instinct to avoid the unpleasant effects of anxiety is so strong that we should not be surprised at how sneaky avoidance can become or how many unexpected forms it may take. As a result, we can easily convince ourselves that we are not avoiding when we are, or fall into a pattern of harmful behaviour in our efforts to avoid the feeling of anxiety.

In this chapter, I will look at some of the ways avoidance can manifest and how it sometimes sneaks into our lives without us realizing it.

Just plain avoiding

The most obvious way we avoid is when we simply don't do something, turning down the invitation to a party, not going into the room with a spider, avoiding driving on motorways and so on. We may find ourselves saying things like 'I never go in lifts' or 'I don't fly in planes; it's not for me.' At least this sort of avoidance is easy to identify! It is simple and honest!

Making excuses and procrastinating

Often, we don't like to think that we are avoiding something completely, but we will find ways around it and keep delaying, deferring or pretending that next time we will act differently. So, when we get an invitation to a party, we tell ourselves that we intend to go, but end up not going this time because we have a headache/are tired/are working tomorrow/have an essay to write. Each of these is a reasonable excuse, but each time the real reason for turning down the invitation is that we feel too anxious about going. Or maybe we know that we need to get out of the house, that physical exercise will do us good, that we always feel better after we have gone for a walk, but anxiety makes us delay and find a reason not to go: it's too early; all the dog-walkers will be out now; I'm a bit tired because I didn't sleep well; I'll go this afternoon; it'll be a bit busy out there now with everyone doing the school run, I'd rather go when it's quieter; oh, look, it's raining! I'll go tomorrow.

Procrastination can be a form of avoiding that is very similar to making excuses. Of course, there are many reasons why people procrastinate, and some have nothing to do with anxiety. For instance, we can procrastinate about a chore we need to do simply because there are so many fun things we'd rather be doing instead, but anxiety is often at the root of procrastination.

When we procrastinate, we don't even have to find an excuse for not doing something, since we are not saying that we won't do it; we will just do it after we've done this, or that. Sometimes it is the idea of the task itself that makes us keep delaying (such as having to make a difficult phone call, for instance), or sometimes a fear of failure so that, subconsciously, we are too fearful to start in case it goes wrong, which might apply to an essay we need to write.

Picking up the phone

Sanjay fully intended to call the surgery to book the blood test. He knew it was overdue as he'd had another text reminder. He'd planned to call on Wednesday, since he'd be finishing work early and would have time, but he was tired after work, and the last thing he had the energy for was phoning the doctor when he got home; he works from home on Thursdays, so he'd do it then instead. There was no point calling first thing in the morning – you know how hard it is to get through to a GP at that time! So he aimed to call mid-morning, but then he was distracted by work, and then when you have a coffee break, you want to be having a break, right? And calling the GP is definitely *not* a break!

He decided to think about it at lunchtime, but worried that the practice might turn the phones off over lunch. Best not to waste time trying; he'd definitely do it in the afternoon. Only he didn't; he deferred, delayed, 'forgot' and then it was half past six and the practice was closed, and another week would go by.

Sanjay wasn't quite sure what made him feel so anxious about calling the GP. It was a combination of things. For starters, he'd never liked phoning anyone – he'd always rather go online or send a text; he hated the phone. And he wasn't that keen on needles either – it wasn't just the idea of all that blood leaving his body; it was knowing that once it was taken, then the results would follow.

He'd have a text or a letter or a call from the GP about the results, and it might not be good news, and he always dreaded that. If you didn't know, then you didn't have to worry. Only he did worry; he worried about the fact that next Thursday he really should call the GP.

Self-medicating

One frequent manifestation of avoidance is not to avoid the activity itself, but to avoid, or at least lessen, the associated anxiety by self-medicating in order to be able to get through it. The most common way of doing this is with alcohol. The calming effect of alcohol is nothing new – the expression 'Dutch courage' comes from the 17th century, when the English were fighting the Dutch and learned that the Dutch spirit, gin, was very useful for calming the nerves before battle. I'm sure people have used alcohol to calm anxiety for as long as they have been able to manufacture it, and in the short term it can be very effective. It's worth thinking about it: is this a bad thing to do?

On the one hand, you can see that it might be helpful. After all, I am arguing that the problem with avoidance is that the more you avoid, the more powerful it becomes, and that what you need to do is to stop avoiding, face your fear and manage your anxiety when you confront the fear, so that the fear lessens its hold on you. With alcohol, you may be able to face a fear rather than running away from it, and to manage the anxiety in the presence of it, so perhaps this is a good thing.

The problem with this approach is three-fold. The first is the very obvious problem of the destructive effects of alcohol. If you need to drink a lot in order to face your fear, then you are exposed to all the risks of hazardous drinking, and if you need to drink regularly to avoid your fear, then you are likely to end up with alcohol dependency. When I think of my patients who have a problem with alcohol, very few have got there through simply wanting to have too much fun; far more common is a long habit of self-medicating in order to cope with crippling anxiety.

The second problem is the depressant effect of alcohol. In moderation, and in the short term, the disinhibiting effects of alcohol can lift the mood and calm anxiety, and so it is hard to see how alcohol acts as a depressant. True, we have all seen how some people slump into a real low when they have had too much to drink, but that doesn't happen all the time, and might never happen to you; far more problematic, and universal, is the *overall* impact on mood. The fact is that people who drink to improve their mood in the short term will have a lower overall mood, and a higher overall level of anxiety than if they did not drink. The analogy I like is to imagine that we have a finite number of 'happy tokens' in a week, and that when we drink, it uses some of them up all at once, lifting our mood in the short term, but leaving us short of happy tokens for the rest of the week when we are sober.

The third problem is that overcoming anxiety is all about regaining the power that anxiety has taken from you, and even if alcohol were a harmless, risk-free placebo, the fact that it is the *alcohol* that is helping you overcome your anxiety does nothing to empower you in mastering it. You have not learned anything about your own inner strength, have not discovered techniques for soothing your anxiety or gained the belief that you can overcome it on your own; it is only you *and* alcohol that can do this. This is why any form of 'medication' that you might take for its immediate calming effect on anxiety is problematic, whether it is alcohol, recreational drugs, homeopathic remedies or a doctor's prescription. The allure of a pill or potion that can overcome anxiety is very attractive, and doctors will sometimes prescribe medication such as beta-blockers or diazepam for this, but all the evidence is that, apart from very occasional use, this approach is unhelpful at best and harmful at worst; even if it works in the short term, it is not a strategy to recommend.

Longer-term medications, such as antidepressants, are a different prospect. These will be discussed in detail in Chapter 18, but suffice to say here that, despite their name, antidepressants do have a place in helping with anxiety. They certainly have both advantages and disadvantages to consider, but the crucial difference is that they are attempting to help with the underlying issue of anxiety, rather than to make someone feel calm when they take them, so that when you do face up to your anxiety, you are becoming empowered to master it on your own terms, not just by the power of a pill or potion.

Obsessive compulsive disorder (OCD)

Adjusting the radio

Julie always felt better with even numbers; there was something unsettling about an odd number, something left over, asymmetrical, awkward. And so she liked to do things in twos; check the front door twice, or sometimes four times; take 12 steps to the car where Manoj, her lift-share, would be waiting. Sometimes he would hover in a different space, but she could always adjust her footing to make it work; there was a lot of counting, but that made her calmer, so she didn't mind.

But there was the car radio. They liked to listen to the radio in the morning; it was part of their routine and they would have a good laugh about the presenter or even sing along sometimes. But Manoj always had it turned on when she got in the car; he didn't seem to care about the volume control. Sometimes it would be on an even number, and she knew it would be a good day, but sometimes the control would be on 7, or, even worse, 9. Why was 9 worse? She didn't know; maybe because it was so close to 10 and even more incomplete than other odd numbers. She would try to ignore it; it was silly, after all. If the dial didn't have numbers, she wouldn't even know! She would close her eyes, but the odd number would burn through the lids, and the unsettled feeling would be so distracting. It wasn't as though she would have a panic attack; she just couldn't relax until it was adjusted. It was exhausting, but she didn't want Manoj to think she was *weird*. She would have to adjust it, subtly, hope he wouldn't notice. If he did, then she'd say she had a headache and it was a bit too loud.

Most of us have rituals or compulsions if we look hard enough. Superstition depends on it – why does someone have to say 'Aye aye, captain' and salute when they see a magpie? Why do we avoid walking under a ladder or touch wood when we wish for something, and why do so many professional footballers have to put their kit on in a certain way before a game? It's because we have associated those things with anxiety; we are left with an unsettled feeling of incompleteness when we see the magpie and don't give it the required salutation – bad luck is said to follow if we fail to complete the ritual, and even if we don't really believe that, it is no big deal to acknowledge the magpie in the time-honoured way, and this instantly relieves us of the anxiety that we might be wishing bad luck on ourselves. Or for the footballer, if they always put their left leg into their shorts before their right, and have associated this with having a good game, then failing to do so will leave them anxious that they might have a bad game – and this distraction might actually follow them on to the pitch, so that they do indeed have a bad game because it affects their focus, and so it is easier to take their shorts off and put them on the right way.

But this is not OCD.

These minor rituals are part of normal human existence, and while they might be annoying, they have little impact on our lives. OCD is when these rituals become a major way of controlling our anxiety and start to dominate our lives. When someone says they are 'a bit OCD' because they like their pencils lined up neatly on their desk, they are trivializing what can be a life-controlling condition that cripples and exhausts people with the demands it makes upon them. Sometimes the OCD seems to come out of nowhere, but usually it arises from a need to manage generalized anxiety. Especially if the anxiety is something that we can't avoid and can't control, then it makes sense that we might turn to ways of trying to soothe ourselves from our anxiety. The allure of OCD is that it promises to bring a sense of calm when the ritual or compulsion is followed, but the very short-term nature of this effect means that we have to keep performing the rituals or compulsions, which have a tendency to add on to one another and escalate, ensnaring us in the process.

Once we remember that it is the *feelings of anxiety* we are desperate to avoid, it is easy to see how avoidance is a key part of OCD, since it is by conforming to certain patterns or rituals that a temporary lessening of anxiety is achieved. Learning to achieve peace while not doing the rituals is possible and involves all the same principles as any type of anxiety, but OCD can be especially

challenging since the rituals can become so ingrained in everyday life.

Harm OCD

It is worth saying something about harm OCD here because it is
not well enough understood, even by healthcare professionals,
and can be a very lonely and bewildering journey. As well as compulsions to do rituals that reduce anxiety, another feature of OCD
can be intrusive thoughts that lead to obsessional ways of thinking.
The more startling these intrusive thoughts are, the more anxiety they provoke and the more we might seek to avoid the associated anxiety in ways that encourage the thoughts to stick around,
which is the spiralling cycle that occurs in harm OCD.

If we were to have the random thought 'What if I see a squirrel
today?' it is unlikely to provoke an anxious reaction (let us assume
that we do *not* have sciurophobia!) and so the thought will pass
quickly through our mind, and we will move on. However, if the
thought 'What if I kill someone today?' pops into our head, then
the reaction could be very different. Weird, bizarre and unpleasant thoughts like this are perfectly normal, and most people have
them intrude into our consciousness from time to time, but we
just think, 'What a horrid thought', and dismiss it like we delete
junk mail in our email inbox. But what would happen if we started
to doubt ourselves and worry that maybe we *really could* kill someone? Harm OCD is where this happens, and someone becomes
obsessionally worried that they might be capable of harm, either
in general or to a specific person (such as their children or partner), or to themselves, anxiously worrying that they might take
their own life. Absolutely key to harm OCD is that the very idea of
doing harm in this way is horrifying to the person affected. This
is not someone with an anger problem who realizes they might

be a danger, or someone with suicidal thoughts who is actually considering ending their life, nor is it a person with fixed delusional thoughts as might be seen in psychosis. It is the horrifying nature of how someone feels about these thoughts that raises their anxiety to extreme levels and, you guessed it, leads to avoidance behaviour that reinforces the obsession.

The avoidance in harm OCD is usually two-fold. The most common is when the affected person seeks reassurance that they are not violent, which acts in a similar way to reassurance in health anxiety as described in the next chapter. The extreme anxiety that they might be capable of violence leads to constantly trying to reassure themselves that they are not; this might be checking themselves for violent feelings, asking other people if they think they could be violent, or looking online to find out about the character traits of violent people to check against their own character. This provides temporary relief when they are reassured that they are not capable of violence, but it becomes a self-fulfilling prophecy since they are now thinking about violence a lot of the time – and this reinforces their fear that maybe they are a violent person, after all!

A second form of avoidance in harm OCD is to avoid situations that become perceived as increasing the risk of the feared violent behaviour, such as locking the drawer that contains the kitchen knives, avoiding shops that sell knives or places where violence could take place. This more obvious avoidance limits the more mundane associations with these situations, so that a kitchen knife, for instance, only becomes linked in the mind with violence and no longer with chopping vegetables.

In my experience, harm OCD is not solely related to the idea of violence but can occur with any intrusive thought that is linked with anxiety and is upsetting to someone as it clashes with their nature. I am aware of cases where someone has become obsessed with the worry that they might be a paedophile, when they clearly have no tendencies this way, or extreme anxiety about the possibility of suicide when they have no wish whatsoever to harm themselves. Unfortunately, harm OCD is little talked about, even in medical circles, which frequently leaves those affected very isolated and often misunderstood. People affected frequently feel like they are monsters; they are not! Once you understand it, it is very easy to recognize what is happening with harm OCD and we should talk more about it.

Eating disorders

While the exact cause of eating disorders is very complex, and far beyond the scope of this book, an essential driver behind an eating disorder is also the relief of anxiety. Frequently, a person with an eating disorder is in a stressful situation that they can't avoid and over which they feel little ability to control. This might be family tensions, issues with self-worth, anxiety about the future or any manner of other stresses, and it is important to not over-simplify the situation or to imply that the underlying issues will be easy to identify. If you assume, though, that there might be issues that cause stress and lead to a feeling of being out of control, it is not surprising that someone might try to regain a sense of control by exerting influence over one area they can control – how and when they eat. Restricting eating, or purging after eating, is all about control and the lessening of anxiety when this control is achieved. The feeling of anxiety is avoided by strict control over the person's relationship with food, with all of its destructive consequences.

Self-harm

Self-harm, in the form of cutting, for instance, is often described by those who do it as a way of releasing tension. There is something about physical pain that seems able to do this; it distracts from the cause of the tension, probably releases endorphins and other hormones that affect how we feel, and can make people feel calmer. Again, the short-term result is to reduce the feeling of anxiety, but the long-term impact is destructive; there are many complex issues involved with self-harm, but once more the avoidance of anxiety plays a significant role.

Seeking reassurance

Anxiety is often characterized by the question 'What if?'– 'What if I miss my train?', 'What if I mess up at work?', 'What if I fail my exams?' – and we might find ourselves trying to avoid the feeling of anxiety that these 'What ifs' cause by seeking reassurance. For instance, we might ask those around us if they think we will fail our exam, or whether we are good enough at our job. And because the relief we feel when they reassure us that we will be okay is only temporary, we have to keep seeking that reassurance.

Seeking reassurance is especially significant in health anxiety. Since it is impossible to avoid our own body when it gives us symptoms that worry us, seeking reassurance is the obvious place to go. Health anxiety is a big subject, and so I have dedicated the whole of the next chapter to the topic. Here, it will suffice to say that the actions taken by someone affected by health anxiety – seeking reassurance, visiting the doctor, checking symptoms on Google – might seem too active to be a form of avoidance. After all, when someone with health anxiety seeks reassurance, they are not avoiding seeing the doctor. But seeking reassurance is exactly about avoiding – avoiding the feeling of anxiety associated with worrying about your health. And, like all the other methods of avoidance, it works in the short term, but its calming effects are very brief, and the long-term impact can be very difficult to live with.

Finding another way

Reading this chapter, you may conclude that you are not allowed to avoid your anxiety, but there is nothing wrong with wanting the feelings of anxiety to go away! Ultimately, the whole purpose of this book is that it might help you reduce feelings of anxiety, and this is a good thing. The problem with all the above ways of avoiding, however, is not only the restrictive and destructive impact they can have on our lives, but the fact that they all tend to make anxiety strengthen its grip on us; they take power from us rather than giving it to us. If we are to truly master anxiety, then we need to challenge the natural, and powerful, inclination to avoid and instead find another way, which will be covered in detail in the third part of this book. If you are in a hurry to get there, then you can skip straight to that section now; otherwise, we will take a moment to talk about health anxiety before tackling the important subject of burnout.

Chapter 7

Health anxiety

A particularly tricky beast!

Every GP has a number of patients affected by health anxiety, some quite mildly and others so significantly that it dominates their lives because it can be so uniquely challenging to live with. And yet I have never been to a lecture where I have been taught about health anxiety, I struggle to know how to record it on the GP record – there is no medical code for 'health anxiety' on GP computer systems – and there aren't any guidelines for how to treat it. For all these reasons, I thought health anxiety deserved a whole chapter of its own!

The National Institute for Health and Care Excellence (NICE) is the main body that produces clinical guidelines in the UK and it usually has a guideline for everything. It does have one for anxiety, and the summary states that:

> It covers a range of anxiety disorders, including generalised anxiety disorder, social anxiety disorder, post-traumatic stress disorder, panic disorder, obsessive-compulsive disorder and body dysmorphic disorder.

There is no mention of health anxiety. Searching the full document, the phrase 'health anxiety' yields zero results.[6] The old (and unhelpful) term for health anxiety is hypochondriasis, and NICE has not produced a guideline for this either.

I genuinely do not know why this is. I suspect it has something to do with the fact that people with health anxiety are only very rarely treated by psychiatrists, and it is usually specialists who write guidelines and not GPs. I think it is a wider societal issue, though, since it is even hard to find online support for health anxiety; there seems to be little in the way of any network where people help each other with this problem.

Whatever the reason, I think it means people with health anxiety are poorly served by both the medical profession and wider society. Medicine excels at investigating and treating physical disease, but it is less well equipped for what to do when all the tests are normal. As a doctor, it is easy to reassure the patient and fail to tackle the underlying problem of health anxiety. In the meantime, the government, well-meaning celebrities and single-disease charities engage in awareness-raising campaigns that tell us all to 'check your breasts', 'look for blood in your pee or your poo', 'see a doctor about your prostate', 'get a cough checked out if it lasts three weeks' or 'trust your instinct', and 'if something is telling you that your body is not right, it is always best to see a doctor and get it checked'. There is no recognition that these advertising campaigns can be a nightmare for someone with health anxiety to navigate, and no advert telling you what to do if health anxiety is your problem. I hope this will change one day.

Definitions

So what is health anxiety? Since there is no clear guideline, it is hard to give an official definition. The old term, hypochondriasis, is highly problematic. First, it is a term that makes no sense in the 21st century. It literally means 'under the ribs', because in times gone by it was believed that melancholy (depression and other mental health problems) originated from bile and was located in the upper abdomen. Second, there have been so many jokes and stereotypes made about *the hypochondriac*, from Molière's play of 1673 to the present day, that the term is laden with stigma and ridicule.

In America, the term 'illness anxiety disorder' is used in preference, but this has not come into use in the UK and, in my opinion, defines something much rarer than the health anxiety I see in patients so often in the GP surgery. It is indeed defined as being a very rare condition and describes an illness where someone is convinced they are unwell to an almost delusional extent, despite repeated medical evidence to the contrary. This does exist, but it is certainly rare; I have only seen it a couple of times in my career.

What I see far more frequently is people who become overly anxious about their health, misinterpret minor symptoms as being signs of serious disease and live in fear of discovering they have a serious physical condition, with cancer or heart disease usually being top of the list. They are not deluded, they are happy to be reassured and believe what their doctor says, but the worry keeps coming back. It is also important to note that sometimes the anxiety is more apparent by proxy, where the worry is about the health of a loved one (most commonly a parent worrying excessively about the health of their child).

What makes health anxiety different

Many aspects of health anxiety are similar to all experiences of anxiety; the sweaty palms, racing heart and tendency to panic are all the same. There are two aspects of health anxiety, however, that make it very different and uniquely challenging.

The first is that you can't run away from it like you can with other anxieties. If you are scared of spiders, you can get yourself away from the spider in order to feel better (we have already discussed how this may not be the best strategy, but at least it is an option). When your anxiety is about your health, how do you avoid that? You can't run away from your own body! And so people with health anxiety end up finding unique ways to avoid feeling anxious, primarily through seeking reassurance, which we will come to.

The second challenge with being anxious about your health is that anxiety creates physical symptoms, and since it is physical symptoms that you worry about, this simply adds fuel to the fire. The more anxious you become, the more you will experience those symptoms, and so the more convinced you will be that there really is something wrong, and the more anxious you will be as a result. For anyone with anxiety, it can help to gain an understanding of the physical symptoms of anxiety, but when it is your health that you worry about, this becomes essential. You need to be able to correctly interpret the symptoms your body is giving you as a result of being anxious, in order to slow down the vicious cycle between anxiety and physical symptoms.

Reassurance seeking

Excessively seeking reassurance is one of the hallmarks of health anxiety. This may be by constantly checking your own body: keeping track of your pulse with your fitness device, for instance, or constantly examining yourself for lumps. It may involve checking with relatives or friends, asking them over and over what they think until they start to become irritated with you. Or it could involve going to the doctor when most people would not, or asking the doctor to do tests 'just in case'. Clearly, there are many circumstances where it is entirely right to be worried about symptoms and to seek medical advice, and we will come to that when we talk about the role of a symptom filter below, but what is key about reassurance-seeking behaviour in health anxiety is that it brings relief to the symptoms of the anxiety, but that the relief is only temporary; it is the same as avoidance.

What if?

Jack felt so much better after seeing the doctor; it was almost palpable how much weight had shifted from his shoulders, and he felt good as he walked back to work. There was nothing serious; there was no lump that the doctor could find and he didn't have cancer.

Later that day, however, the doubt began to creep back in. It was odd, wasn't it, that the doctor didn't seem able to find the lump when it was so obvious to Jack? Well, it wasn't always obvious; sometimes he couldn't find it either, but it was definitely there. What if the doctor hadn't examined him properly? What if he had missed the lump and it really was serious? Shouldn't he have been offered a scan? He'd heard that doctors could miss lumps and they turned out to be cancer months later and then it was too late.

Jack took a break from his desk and went to the bathroom to check himself again. The lump was there. The doctor must have missed it. He'd have to go back; better to ask for a scan this time.

Sometimes reassurance can be effective, at least until the next symptom comes along, but usually its effects wear off very quickly, the anxiety levels start to build again, doubts and 'what ifs' crowd in, and the need to seek reassurance once more becomes unbearable.

In its worst form, reassurance seeking can become almost like an addiction and the need to regularly feed the habit takes over. It is the only real form of avoidance behaviour that is open to someone with health anxiety, and like other forms of avoidance behaviour, it is hard to resist, but only makes the problem worse.

A broken symptom filter

How, then, does someone with health anxiety know when they really should see a doctor? Here, it can help to imagine that we all have a symptom filter, something in our brain that helps us to pay attention to important symptoms while ignoring ones that don't matter. It is key that we all have this ability, since our bodies present us with symptoms all the time. Right now, as I write this, I have a variety of different symptoms that I am ignoring. For no apparent reason, I have an itch on both my right shoulder and my left shin, while the tingling in my right foot is because I have my foot tucked under my other leg while I work. I have a mild ache in both my shoulders from too much computer work, and because the room is very quiet with only the steady tick of a clock to break the silence, I have mild ringing tinnitus in both my ears.

All of these symptoms are being filtered out for now. I will have to scratch one of the itches if they persist, and I will move my leg before the tingling gets too much; if the tinnitus gets annoying, I will put some quiet music on, and I will get up and stretch soon to relieve the ache in my shoulders, but none of it is stimulating a sense of anxiety; my symptom filter is happy that they are all trivial and no alarm bells are ringing.

However, if I had health anxiety, then my symptom filter may be broken. I may have a heightened awareness of symptoms so that I find them hard to ignore and my mind starts overthinking. What if the tingling is a sign of multiple sclerosis? What if the shoulder ache is more than that? Isn't there a condition I have heard of where shoulder pains can be serious? Polymyalgia, I think it's called, and it's linked to suddenly going blind, or so I've read. What if the tinnitus is a brain tumour?

When you have health anxiety, it can help to think of your symptom filter being broken; you need to recalibrate it, learning what most people would do if they had these symptoms, almost starting from scratch with what should be checked out and what can be ignored, and learning that instinct is not always right and cannot always be trusted.

The danger of confirmation bias

I have talked previously about confirmation bias, and it can play a major role in health anxiety. This form of bias is where we pay more attention to facts that support our previously held views and prejudices, and discount those that contradict what we already believe.

With health anxiety, confirmation bias means that we will be prone to giving too much weight to health scares and tragic stories of missed diagnoses or people diagnosed with serious illness at a young age. If a close friend or relative is diagnosed with a serious condition or dies at a young age, this can have a major impact; even stories in the news of a celebrity being diagnosed with cancer or seeing a health awareness campaign poster at a bus stop can send health anxiety out of control. Words like 'cancer' in the news headlines stand out as though they are written in huge red letters, and even our favourite soap opera makes us worry as yet another character gets the diagnosis. And yet we ignore or discount evidence that tells the opposite story. We may know, for instance, that our personal risk of cancer is very low, or that heart disease is highly unlikely in a 30-year-old non-smoker who looks after their health, or the constant everyday evidence that most people spend years of their life in remarkably good health.

Google is a snare, wearable devices are a quagmire

Modern technology is not kind to people with health anxiety. The internet is a valuable source of information, and if you need specific information about a health condition, it can be fantastic. If your doctor gives you a diagnosis, for instance, and you need to go and learn about your condition, then, as long as you go to a reliable website, you can find out all you need to know.

Googling symptoms, however, is like playing roulette. I often say to patients that we are only six clicks from cancer on the internet. It is very tempting, when you are worried about your health, to have a quick check on the internet, and sometimes you will get reassurance when you search for the cause of your symptoms, but it is rather like gambling. Sometimes you lose straight away, sometimes you win, but stay on there too long and you always lose, and the trouble is that it is always tempting to stay too long. It might be that when you first type in your symptoms, you will get some relief; there is a simple explanation and you don't need to worry. But it is always tempting to just check one more time, and you only need one website that tells you that you *should* worry for it to all go spiralling out of control.

And as for wearable devices? It doesn't take much thinking to realize

that the last thing a person with health anxiety needs is the ability to constantly check their pulse rate!

Where has it come from?

If you are affected by health anxiety, it may be helpful to consider where it has come from. Have you always felt this way? Is it part of how you were brought up? Is it because other people around you also worry about their health? Or maybe they don't worry enough, and you subconsciously feel you have to do the worrying for everyone! Maybe it started with a health scare or a serious illness in someone close to you.

There may be no obvious reason why you have health anxiety, but if there is, then it can be helpful to understand this. It may be some strongly held cultural beliefs that you hold that seem so obvious that you have never thought to challenge them. For instance, one belief which is rarely questioned in our society is that it is always better to know what is going on in your body. This seems self-evident, but it is not true. It is often better to know, of course, if there is something serious going on, but sometimes the quest to know everything leads to more problems. We are not machines that can be easily taken apart, repaired and put back together again; many tests done by doctors carry risks, or might turn up something that just makes you more worried, like an incidental finding on a scan that turns out to be nothing, but has to be looked into further.

Sometimes it can even be better not to know about a serious diagnosis like cancer. For instance, about half the men who die aged 80 have prostate cancer, if you look closely enough at their prostates at post-mortem. But these are men who never had an illness caused by prostate cancer and never knew they had it; they died with it, not of it. Sometimes ignorance really is bliss, and this can be hard to navigate in medicine. There have been whole books written on the subject of medical overdiagnosis, but it is sufficient here to simply challenge the mantra that knowing is always best.

Seek help

Although some people with health anxiety actively avoid seeing a doctor for fear of what they might find, most people affected by it will be used to seeing a doctor, or going to the hospital emergency department, but they won't be used to seeking help about health anxiety. This is because the physical symptoms always get in the way; they are what drives someone to go to the doctor, and the need for reassurance dominates the consultation. Even if someone chooses to attend to talk about their anxiety, there is a fair chance that a physical concern will pop up by the time of the appointment, and the urge to talk about it will be so strong that it will distract from the need to talk about the anxiety, sometimes hijacking the appointment entirely.

If you are to get help with the anxiety, you will need to develop a consistent relationship with a doctor you can trust: someone who can help you recalibrate your symptom filter, who can protect you from over-investigation and a plethora of referrals to specialists, but who will know when to do tests and refer when it is the right thing to do. And you will need to make an appointment and suppress the urge to talk about physical symptoms but allow the focus to be on how to manage your anxiety, how to gain the skills to hold your symptoms in perspective, and to discuss the role of therapy and even medication in order to stop it dominating your life.

Part 2

Burnout

You can't get better if you
are running on empty

Chapter 8

I'm not the sort of person to get burnout

What has happened to me?

Broken

Samir had never been anxious in his life. He was a doer, a fixer, Mr Reliable, the go-to man for your problems. He worked hard, took responsibility, cared for his family; in the busy season, he would stay late, get the job done and meet the deadline.

The panic attack occurred on the commute to London, but it was nothing to do with the train. It was the looming shadows and sounds of London, the office getting closer with every rattle on the tracks, familiar buildings passing the windows. Pressure built in his chest.

He was sure he was having a heart attack; it was in his family, after all, and the tightness in his chest was just as he had always imagined it would be. He suppressed it on the train; St Thomas' Hospital was right near Waterloo. Somehow, he got himself there, sweating profusely, struggling with every breath. He was relieved to make it and glad when they told him there was nothing wrong; they'd run all the tests, his heart was fine, his lungs were perfect. But he was left bewildered by what had happened. And as he made his way home, why did he feel his chest tighten again when he looked at the emails on his phone?

Sometimes the cause of our anxiety is far from obvious. There is no one situation that precipitates it, no single thing we are fearful of, no obvious event that triggered it. We just feel tense and anxious all the time, overwhelmed and unable to cope. There are many causes of this, but one of the most common is burnout. And when it happens to you all at once, blindsiding you like nothing you have ever experienced before, it is almost always burnout.

Burnout is not a medical diagnosis, but it is a useful concept since it is quite intuitive as to what it means; it indicates that we have become overloaded. The final trigger is usually trivial – the simple commute to work, a minor argument, bad news that we would normally take in our stride – but today, on this occasion, it floors us like we've been hit by an express train. The straw has broken the camel's back.

An analogy I use to explain burnout is to think about a stress fracture. If someone goes on a very long march, there is a chance that they might sustain a stress fracture in one of the long bones in the foot. This fracture does not result from falling over at some specific point in the march, but is caused by the continual pounding, step after step, until the fracture occurs. The stress fracture may only become apparent once the march is over and they start to realize that the pain is not just an ache from all that exertion. Within a short while, someone who was able to march many miles finds that they cannot even walk a few steps without pain. And so it is with burnout. It is the continual pounding that causes the problem; repeated, unrelenting pressure gradually builds over a prolonged period of time until something snaps. It might be a panic attack as happened in the example with Samir, or it might be bursting into tears, not being able to face going to work or feeling overwhelmed when thinking about your emails. The issue is the same, since the person who previously did so much and functioned so well now finds they cannot function at all.

The nature of burnout is brilliantly explored by Dr Tim Cantopher in his excellent book *Depressive Illness: The Curse of the Strong.*[7] It is probably the book I recommend to patients more than any other, for the simple reason that people who burn out are often utterly bewildered that it has happened to them: 'I'm not the sort of person who gets depressed!' they say to me, while I am thinking that they are *exactly* the sort of person to get depressed! They will have a lot to learn about burnout, depression and anxiety, and Cantopher's book is hugely valuable to them. Cantopher calls it a depressive illness, and he is not wrong, but, in my experience, usually anxiety is also a prominent feature of burnout.

The reason why so many people who get burnout fail to recognize it is that society still has huge stigmas and prejudices against mental illness. Many people see depression or anxiety as a sign of weakness, and so conclude that a strong person shouldn't get depressed. And yet, when it comes to burnout, you have to be a strong person to carry that load.

The key thing about camels and straws is that camels can carry very heavy loads; they are not weak – they are strong! The classic person who gets burnout is a strong person; they work hard, set high standards and solve other people's problems. Often, they are the hub of the family, the reliable person to whom everyone turns; when things get hard, they don't stop – they just pedal harder. They care about what they do and are not good at delegating, either because they think the only way to do it properly is to do it yourself, or out of a sense of duty and not wanting to put upon someone else. Frequently, they work in the caring professions or in a highly responsible, high-pressure job, or they may not be in paid work but have high levels of caring responsibilities within the family. They might have elderly parents who need increasing levels of help, or a child with complex needs, or often both. Crucially, people who burn out are not armour-coated; they care what people think about them, they want to do a good job and like to be liked, and so they are vulnerable to criticism, with self-criticism often being the hardest of all to manage.

Mood homeostasis

Another way of thinking about what happens in burnout is to consider what usually happens when we have a period of stress. The natural tendency is for our mood to be affected, but then to bounce back. The body really likes doing this in almost every bodily system; it likes to return everything to normal, and the medical word for this is 'homeostasis', which is from the Greek and simply means 'staying the same'.

Homeostasis is what keeps our body healthy, and it occurs in everything – from how our body regulates temperature, to sugar levels, thyroid levels, hydration status and so on. Whenever something causes any one of these systems to change, we have processes – hormones, behavioural changes, nerve impulses and so on – that all aim to put it back to where it was. So it should not surprise us that mood operates in a similar way. When something stressful happens – or something exciting, for that matter – our mood will be affected for a while, but within a day or two, a week at the most, it will usually be back to baseline.

With our physical systems, however, sometimes our homeostatic mechanisms can break. A clear example of this is diabetes, where the usually tight regulation we have for blood sugar levels no longer works properly and sugars can rise unchecked. The mechanisms for how this happens with mood are a lot more complex than sugar regulation, but we can see the same thing happening. The tendency to bounce back to baseline is broken by the continual pounding, without sufficient time or systems in place to recover between the stresses. It is as if a point of no return has been reached; something has broken.

In Figure 8.1, we can see how this might look. The line charts someone's mood over time, and the arrows mark episodes of stress. Originally, there is good recovery and bounce back because the stresses are spaced apart, but the stresses keep coming and are closer together. There is less opportunity for recovery between the episodes; the body keeps trying to recover, until a point of no return has been reached and the person feels overwhelmed. They are like a spring that has been overstretched and has lost its ability to return to its usual shape. Recovery is certainly possible, but it is not going to happen in a hurry and help will be needed.

Figure 8.1: Mood homeostasis and stress

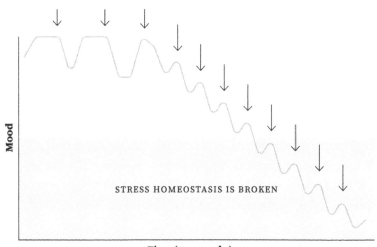

Good stress, bad stress and too much stress

This is not to say that stress is always a bad thing. There is such a thing as good stress, the sort of stress that gets us up in the morning, is invigorating and exciting, and gives us a feeling of satisfaction when we manage it well.

Another useful diagram to consider is Figure 8.2. This is a chart of how performance (how well we function both at home and at work) changes with stress. If we have no stress at all, then we don't perform well, since we have nothing to perform for. As we start to get some stress, then we perform better and start to thrive as we reach the top of the line. Soon after this point, however, our performance no longer increases with more stress, and it levels out, even dropping slightly, but we can still perform well. This stage can last a long time, where we are functioning, but our performance has plateaued; increasingly, we are no longer thriving, but are merely surviving. The danger in this stage is that everything seems okay on the outside; we are hitting our deadlines, achieving our goals and holding the family together; it is most likely that nobody will notice the difference.

At this point, if we can recognize the stress we are under and do something about it – and we will cover this in detail in Chapter 10 – then we can start to go back along the plateau and thrive once more. If we do not notice the warning signs, however, then one day, often without warning, we will find ourselves falling. Often, the falling stage happens with little or no warning; it is like falling off a cliff, and we may find ourselves in a crumpled heap at the cliff base, wondering what on earth has happened.

Figure 8.2: Stress and performance

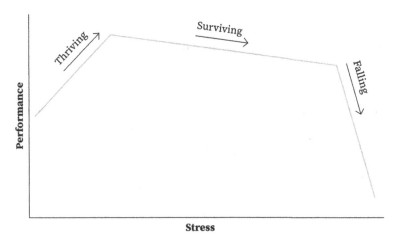

We mustn't confuse stress with hard work. You may be working very hard but loving it and, far from burning out, you may be thriving, since it energizes you. On the other hand, you may not have enough work and that might be a big part of your stress. There may be things in your life that others would find unbearably stressful, but which you take in your stride, while some seemingly small responsibility weighs you down far more than it should.

Recognizing yourself

By far the most viewed post on my Instagram page is the one I did on burnout. At the time of writing, it has had over 4 million views. I try to keep up with the comments on my posts as I love that interaction with people and learn a great deal from how they respond to what I am saying. When this particular post took off, in a way that only the Instagram algorithms truly understand, the comments were coming in so fast one weekend that I was in danger of burnout trying to keep up with them!

Eventually, the irony hit home and I listened to my own words, slowed down and told myself it would be okay if I didn't respond to every single comment! What was interesting about the comments, though, was the huge number of people who felt the post was describing them exactly; they weren't sure whether to laugh or cry about it, but 'I feel seen!' was a common reaction. And, not surprisingly, the next most common reaction was to say: 'This is me, but what do I *do* about it?!' This is such an important question that the next three chapters are going to look at answering it in detail, but here are two important principles to start us off.

Learn about it with an open mind

When I recommend Tim Cantopher's book, I am always encouraged by how many people get hold of a copy and read it. Maybe it is not surprising; they are so keen to understand what on earth has gone wrong that they will do almost anything that might help. Most are almost spookily astonished by how well the book describes them (some have even had to put it down as they were so unnerved by this!), and that is the first part of managing burnout – to learn about it and challenge your prejudices, to realize that it may be your very strength which makes you both a great person to be around but also vulnerable to burnout, and to acknowledge that this is okay.

Seek help

If you are the sort of person I have described, then you are not a natural at seeking help! This is the first step to recovery, however, and your doctor is often the best place to start. You don't need to know what the doctor will be able to do – you may even doubt they can do anything – but just go anyway.

If you have never had a mental health problem before, you may think this isn't the sort of thing to see a GP about; you are used to seeing them when you've got a cough or hurt your back, but for this? You're not sure that people see their doctor about something like this.

Maybe it would help to know that around 25–40 per cent of a typical GP day involves helping people with their mental health. We will have seen a lot more of this than you think and won't be thrown by it. And it always amazes me how just seeing a GP and talking about burnout can start the road to recovery even before we consider any actual treatment. There is something so therapeutic about acknowledging there is a problem and deciding to do something about it. Even before you have any idea how to solve whatever led to you getting burnout, have no clue about what next steps to take and are totally ignorant about treatments for burnout, just knowing that you are not alone and are going to do *something* can make a surprising difference.

What might that something look like? What might the doctor suggest and what steps can you take on your road to recovery?

These are all important questions and we will start looking at them in the next chapter.

Chapter 9

I'm signed off with burnout

What do I do now?

I guess a week wouldn't be so bad

'Maybe I do need a bit of time off, perhaps a week,' Sacha told herself at last. 'Yes, a week, I'll feel better if I have a week off.'

It had taken a long time to get to this place, and she still felt sick in her stomach at the thought of telling work she wasn't going to be in, but she knew she had to do something. She worried about all the tasks in her in-tray and felt bad about dumping on her colleagues; this was the last thing they needed – everyone was so stressed. She didn't know how she would face her boss, or how they would react.

Sacha felt so bad about letting the side down that she convinced herself that it could be just a week; it made it seem less terrible. A week would surely be enough? And yet the thought of what her inbox would look like in a week's time filled her with dread; it was best not to think about that!

If you can relate to what I have just described, you are not alone. Sacha is the conglomeration of the many patients I have met who have had to overcome all manner of internal objections before they got to the point of accepting a sick note. Sometimes the struggles have taken place before they get to my door, and by the time I see them, they have reluctantly concluded that they have no option but to have some time out; at other times, there is still a way to go on this journey.

While there are many similarities, however, everyone's journey is unique. Not everyone needs time off; some people can make changes which are enough to help them find a way forward without a complete break (they sought help when they were still at the 'struggling' stage at the top of the cliff in the last chapter and had not yet reached the 'falling' stage!). For others, taking a complete break is just not possible, since their commitments lie outside the realm of paid work – even in the 21st century, young children and elderly parents are stubbornly reluctant to accept my sick notes and seem to have scant regard for employment law! We have to think more imaginatively to find rest for people in these situations.

For many people, though, time off work is the first and necessary step they have to take. And the question is: what do you do then? You have left the doctors with your note, phoned your boss and explained that you won't be in, but what now? You'd know what to do if you had the flu – you'd take some paracetamol and go back to bed feeling miserable! If you had a broken leg, you would hobble around on crutches, do your exercises and wait for it to heal.

It's not hard to imagine how to manage time off if you were recovering from an operation or appendicitis, but what do you do when you are off with burnout? You don't look ill, you don't feel like going to bed, paracetamol won't help and you have none of the visual cues of illness like crutches or a plaster cast to add validation to being sick. Nor are there any blood tests or scan results you can point to that explain your predicament. You feel exhausted, and your brain is so scrambled it can't focus, which just makes it even harder to know what to do!

Rest

The first thing you may have to do is to rest, and to completely rest. To put your 'out of office' on your emails (or ask someone to do this for you if you can't face doing it yourself), clear your diary of every commitment that seems in any way demanding, leaving in place only those that you will enjoy, take a break from social media and generally hide away, focusing on eating, sleeping, gentle exercise and being with those you love.

If you doubt that total rest might be important as the first step in recovery from burnout, ask yourself what you would do if you had just got home from hospital after a bout of pneumonia or following major surgery. You would rest, and you would spend more time on the sofa watching harmless television than you ever do normally. You would stop thinking about all the tasks you want to achieve, accept help from those who care about you and take time to recover. You may not be able to see your burnout in the same way that you would see a surgical scar on your stomach or leg, but it is no less real and needs to be treated with the same respect.

Once you have rested, you will be able to start seeing the wood for the trees and you will know what steps to take next. And the first of these is to get a better feel for how much time you might need off work in order to recover. I find it very hard to tell the answer to this question the first time I see someone with burnout. I will usually sign them off for one or two weeks and arrange to see them again, and I find it can go one of two ways. Sometimes, a brief period away can make a profound difference; everything is reset, short-term crises have resolved, changes have been made at work and this brief period away is all that has been required.

More often, it is only in stopping that someone realizes just how tired they truly are. The drop in adrenaline that has been propping up a body in crisis unveils the true state of exhaustion that was going on below the surface. Permission to rest seems to have precipitated collapse, but in truth it was happening anyway and it was just a matter of time. The good news is that recovery is the norm, and the outlook is good. It may take time, and at this point I usually expect a minimum of two to three months, often more like six months, away from the work environment, but we can remain optimistic about a full return to being fruitful in the work environment in time.

It might sound scary to hear me talk in months rather than weeks, and, of course, it might not be that long, but it is far better to start a return to work when going back is the next stage of your healing, rather than something you do out of guilt from not being there. Often it is only by fully letting go of work for a while that we can rest, recover and then thrive once we pick it back up again.

Decompress

It is important, as you recover, to remove both the stressful activities that led to burnout and the weight of worry about those activities. You need to be freed from the fear that everything will build up while you are away and be left waiting for you when you return.

I have a recurring dream I get when I am stressed which reminds me of how intense worry about work stresses can be. In my dream, I am trying to start my morning clinic, but things keep interrupting me so that I never get round to calling the first patient. Each time a patient arrives in the waiting room, an 'A' appears by their name on the computer system, indicating that they have arrived, and in my dream the list of 'A's keeps getting longer and longer, never changing to an 'S' for 'seeing' or an 'L' for 'left'!

It would be going too far to describe the dream as a nightmare, but it is certainly not pleasant! If, in my dream, someone were to take me to one side and encourage me to take a half-hour break because I looked stressed, it would only add to the problem, since I would know that even more 'A's would await me after my break. What would help, however, would be if everyone else helped out and started seeing my clinic patients on my behalf. If you are going to have time off with burnout, you need to know that the list of 'A's is not getting longer while you are away. You need to know that your inbox really does not need looking at, that someone else is dealing with your responsibilities and that matters won't be left undealt with until you are back. This may be difficult, because it involves letting go, and that may not be one of your strong points!

It is easy to imagine that we are indispensable, and it is good for both our mental health and our ego to be reminded occasionally

that we are not. I remember a few years ago being under a great deal of pressure with lots on my plate and a hectic week ahead. Every moment of the week was packed with something important that needed to be done, and that I felt I needed to do. I wished I could cancel something, clear some space in my week and feel less stressed, but I had concluded I couldn't pull out of anything as it was all so important, and I had to be there.

Then, on the Monday morning of that exceptionally busy week, I had a call from my brother-in-law in America: there was a major family crisis that turned everything on its head. By Tuesday morning, I was on a flight to the States and every uncancellable item in my diary was cancelled. It was a real learning point for me because everything that had seemed so important went on very well without me! Other people stepped in to fill the gap, or were there anyway, and my role wasn't as vital as it had seemed. It took something genuinely important to show me that I am not indispensable and the entries in my diary are usually not as essential as they might seem.

You will need to reduce the stress you are under, and this will involve looking at your responsibilities outside work as well as in your paid work. It is no use taking time away from paid work if you are still running the local youth football club, heading up the catering at your church or spending hours every week canvassing for a political party! You will need to look at all the different hats you might be wearing and ask yourself three key questions:

1. Is it truly essential that I continue in this role? (Clearly, some roles, like being a parent or a carer, are not roles you can step down from.)
2. Is it a role that gives me energy and may aid my recovery, or a role that drains me? Occasionally, an external role might be very therapeutic for you, but be very discerning before you answer yes to this!

3. If I do need to continue in this role, can I ease the burden of it by asking for help, or by doing it differently?

You will know you have started to decompress when you feel a lightness in your spirit. You may still be exhausted, have anxiety or low motivation, but there will be something of a weight taken off your shoulders – it may be something you haven't felt in a very long while.

Pace yourself

In his book on burnout, Tim Cantopher talks about the 'vacuum cleaner in the middle of the room' sign. He asks his readers what they would do if they were vacuuming the carpet and began to feel drained of energy halfway through the task – would they be able to leave the vacuuming for a while and have a rest to recharge? If so, then he is optimistic that they will do well and are in charge of their recovery. But if not, then he worries that they have not yet got it. And as for those people who would not only have to finish vacuuming the whole room but the whole house as well before they allowed themselves to rest...well they have a lot to work on!

Pacing is important in recovery from any significant illness, whether it is burnout, pneumonia, major surgery or long COVID. If you get pacing wrong, then you overdo things one day and spend the next day recovering, or you are so afraid to overdo it that you fail to rehabilitate and so get out of condition. I like to talk to my patients about the 'rule of 75 per cent'. Imagine that you wake up with a pot of energy every day and make it your goal to use up 75 per cent of that energy throughout the day. That way, if you misjudge it slightly, or something crops up late in the day that needs your attention, you will still have some energy left and will not end up stealing energy from the next day as a form of energy debt. But you will still have done *something*; you won't have only used up 25 per cent of your energy, and in that way you are gently pushing your recovery without overdoing it. You can even imagine dividing the day up into equal parts of energy and aiming to use 75 per cent of each part of the day before you take a break. Each time, you should be able to say to yourself, 'I could have done a bit more, but I would have been tired if I had kept going much longer.'

Guilt

Many people who burn out are influenced in the actions they take by strong feelings of guilt. Guilt is a common emotion to feel, but it is a very poor leader and rarely tells us the right thing to do. It is very different from remorse. Remorse is when we have done something wrong and would like to try to put it right, and it can be a very important guide to how we should act, leading to appropriate apologies, correction of wrongs and restored relationships.

Guilt, however, has a tendency to turn up even when we haven't done anything wrong; it likes to condemn us anyway. Guilt makes us feel bad, often laying responsibilities at our door that are not our fault, and it comes with its equally unhelpful partner in crime, blame. If you burnt out because, as well as working too hard, you were partying every weekend and fuelling your body with drugs to keep up an unsustainable lifestyle, then maybe you need to feel some remorse! But for most of the people who need to read this section of the book, it is enough to say that you may well be feeling guilty, but that does not mean you are to blame.

These are common emotions, and it can help to acknowledge them, but you don't have to follow their lead. Guilt often results in overthinking, catastrophizing and the sort of worry that does not help us get better. When you find yourself feeling bad about what has happened to you and guilty about the impact on others, do acknowledge this, but then shift your focus away from feelings of guilt and on to what is going to help you get better.

Routine is crucial

One of the hardest things about being signed off work is the loss of routine. It is what allows us to rest and recover, since we no longer have to get to work on time, but we can be left floundering with the loss of structure that work usually provides. If you don't have to get up for work on a Monday morning, what time do you get up? And what do you do with yourself when your usually packed diary suddenly becomes empty?

Since routine is so important for wellbeing, one of the most important things to get right as you recover is to try to build this into your week. Set your alarm for a similar time to when you would usually wake up while you were working. Clearly, if your job involves very early starts or shift working, then you will want to adapt this, but try to stick to what would be a sensible time to get up, and avoid the temptation to lie in every day. Once you have the energy to plan your recovery, start putting things in your diary – simple things like a regular walk or other exercise, time to go food shopping or meeting a friend for coffee. This will help to avoid you drifting and will also make it easier for you to do some of the things which you know will help but you might keep putting off. If you wait until you feel like doing some exercise, for instance, then you might be waiting for ever, but if it is in your diary, then there is a greater chance that you will be able to make it happen.

You might want to keep the rhythm of the week and weekends – if you usually have a lie-in at a weekend, for instance, then you might enjoy that while you recover. It might help to keep a sense of the weekly pattern we are so used to, as well as that feeling of enjoying the weekend.

As well as helping give us a sense of order in the day, sticking to a routine is also key to maintaining good sleep. When we have less pressure to get out of bed, it is easy to spend too long in it – either by going to bed too early or sleeping in too late. Our entire sleep pattern can then become disrupted, so that either we lie awake for long, anxious hours in the middle of the night, or else our sleep shifts so that we go to sleep ever later and end up waking up at midday. I will say a lot more about sleep and sleep patterns in Chapter 15, so if this is a big issue for you, then you might want to jump ahead to that chapter before returning here.

Consider therapy

I will cover the topic of talking therapy in Chapter 17. For the moment, I would just like to challenge you to give therapy some serious thought. People often say to me things like 'I don't think I really need therapy' or 'I don't see how talking about things can help.' I think we need to challenge these views! Try not to think about whether you need or deserve therapy. Of course, you will probably get better without it, but it is not a competition and there are no prizes for managing to recover without help. The question to ask yourself is far simpler: would therapy be helpful? And if you have burnout, then the answer to that question is almost certainly yes! You missed the signs that you were burning out, probably have a lot to learn about how to look after yourself without being selfish (which might be one of your biggest fears) and will need guidance about your rehabilitation journey – what's not to like about getting help with that?

And if you can't see how talking therapy can make a difference, then you are not alone – a lot of people say that to me – but reservations about therapy are generally based on a misunderstanding about how intricately our thoughts, feelings and body are connected, and how powerful it can be to gain an understanding of how they operate as a cohesive whole. We can imagine that since we have lived in our mind and body all our lives, we shouldn't need any help with it, but that is a false assumption. If an upcoming tennis prodigy were to say that they knew how to play tennis and so why on earth do they need a coach, we would laugh at their ignorance and advise them to get one anyway! In the same way, if you have never tried talking therapy and are doubtful that it can 'work' then, in the nicest possible way, I would like to challenge you to take a risk and try it anyway!

There may be a role for medication

Chapter 18 is where I will talk about medication in detail; suffice to say here that full recovery from burnout is very possible without taking medication, but sometimes it can be intense and the feeling of being overwhelmed or emotionally drained makes it very difficult to put plans into action. You may know what you need to do to put routine into your week, manage your sleep and engage in therapy, but your brain is simply too frazzled to be able to do it! This is when an antidepressant might have the most to offer, so that it can take down your overall level of symptoms, enabling you to plan what you need for your recovery.

Undertake new activities, ones that help you recover rather than tasks that need to be done

Once you have had an initial period of rest and ensured that you have some space to recover without worrying about your inbox, you can start thinking about what will help you recover. You will need to fill your week with something, but what should that look like? The activities you now fill your time with may look and feel very different to how you used to operate before your burnout. You used to fill your week with tasks that needed to be done, squeezing them in where you could find space in your frantic week. Now, it will be best to undertake activities that help you recover, rather than tasks that need your attention. These might be things that you enjoy doing! It will feel oddly self-indulgent to do things you enjoy while you are off sick, but your duty to your employer is not to feel miserable and delay your recovery, but to do whatever it takes to get better. You will have to get used to the fact that if you go for a walk, or play a game of tennis, you may meet one of your colleagues who may not understand the importance of exercise in recovery, but hiding away at home so that you don't bump into anyone is not going to help.

What these activities might look like is a really important question that has many layers, which is why the whole of the next chapter is dedicated to trying to answer it.

Chapter 10

Burnout recovery

Discover the right side of your brain

If you want to learn how to draw portraits, a really useful exercise is to have a go at drawing them upside down. It doesn't sound like a sensible thing to do, but it is a technique often used by art teachers, especially when teaching someone how to draw portraits.

What is fascinating is that everything is familiar and yet unfamiliar. You know you are drawing an eye, but it doesn't look like an eye and all the lines are going in the wrong direction. To start with, this is unsettling, but once you get over the oddness of doing it, your brain starts to work on the very basic shapes it is seeing; it is able to forget that it is drawing an eye or a nose and concentrates on the length of a line, the way it curves this way or that and the shapes that lie between the lines.

The idea of this is that the left side of the brain tends to want to dominate. It is where our language centre lies; we can imagine it talking all the time, impatiently wanting to get each job done and move on to the next one. When we try to draw something as familiar as a face with the left side of the brain, this linguistic focus and impatient dominance can often cause a great deal of frustration.

The left side of the brain tells us that it knows what an eye looks like, and so we draw what we *think* we should be seeing and not the shapes we can actually see before us. Our knowledge, for instance, tells us that the iris is round, and yet when we look at the real shape of an iris in a portrait, it is almost never round; the top and bottom are almost always cut off by the line of the eyelid. The pupil is also meant to be a perfect circle, yet in real life it usually has a chunk cut out of it by an area of reflected light. The left side of the brain misses these details when it tries to reproduce the drawing, and yet can tell that the drawing 'does not look right', which leads to frustration.

Figure 10.1: The iris and pupils are odd shapes and almost never perfectly round

The right side of the brain can be thought of as more abstract; it is not the centre of language and so is a calmer, more ethereal place which is far better at noticing fine details, such as the curve and length of a line, or the shape of a negative space between two lines. In turning the picture upside down, the left side of the brain no longer recognizes the image as a face, and so it calms down and stops telling us what it thinks we can see; we make room for the right side of the brain, which can focus on the actual lines and shapes we can see, and so we make a more accurate drawing.

I am always cautious about using scientific language to make an argument, since it can just be a lazy way of sounding clever; do the right and left sides of the brain *really* operate in this way? In truth, I don't know; certainly, the left side of the brain is usually the centre of language while the right side of the brain is more important for spatial awareness; beyond that, I am uncertain, but it doesn't matter. What I can say, however, as an amateur artist who particularly likes drawing portraits, is that it feels a bit like my brain has two modes. There are times when I am drawing when I know I am thinking too much and being impatient, and others when I have gone into 'the zone' and relaxed into the drawing, when all I am focusing on are the lines and the shapes, and that is when I am both at my most relaxed and at my best as an artist.

Whatever we think about the scientific basis of being in the right or left side of our brain, what we can say is that there are different experiences of how we feel our brain is working. Sometimes it is rushed and full of anxious thoughts (or stimulating thoughts – we should not just think of the left side of our brain as being a bad place!) and at other times it seems to slow down, as we focus on the finer details of what we are doing.

This 'right side of the brain' feeling is characterized by being absorbed by something that takes our full attention and we often lose track of time; it is hard to worry about things when we are in this zone, because our brain is too occupied in the task at hand to think about anything else. In fact, if you told us to think about something that was worrying us, we probably wouldn't be able to – we would lose our train of thought as we get lost in the task that has our attention. We are likely to forget to turn the oven on, or leave it on too long, or miss an appointment when we are in a right-brain activity. If we are due to pick the children up from school, it is best that we set an alarm so that we don't leave them stranded at the school gate!

What we can also say is that when we allow ourselves to get lost in something like this, it can have a profound effect on our mood. It is soothing and helps us to forget our worries for a time, and so have a rest from them. It helps us to stop ruminating and catastrophizing, making us look outwards rather than inwards at our problems. All in all, it does us good! So the question is this: what are your right-brain activities?

Learning to identify, practise and celebrate these right-brain activities can be particularly important in helping to manage generalized anxiety, where anxiety is not limited to a particular situation or trigger but is our constant companion whatever we are doing. Generalized anxiety may be something we have always known and lived with or may be a feature of burnout. So how do we find the way into the right side of our brain?

Finding your right-brain activities

The defining characteristic of a right-brain activity is that you get lost in it, that when you engage in it, you struggle to think of anything else and you feel soothed by doing it. This will be different for different people, and it certainly won't always be art!

For one of the GPs I worked with for many years, it was always being outdoors and usually involved running or cycling. She would completely lose herself as she ran outdoors, often losing track not only of time but even of where she had run to! She wouldn't be able to tell you what she had been thinking about, other than just how good it was to be outside doing exercise.

I trained for the marathon once, many years ago, and when I went running, I spent most of my time being bored! I would struggle to know what to think about, and my mind would default to working out how far I had run, how quickly I was going, how long the rest of the run would take me, what time I would complete the marathon if I kept at this rate and so on. I was definitely stuck in the left side of my brain! I'm not saying that running did not do me good, but it didn't rest my brain in the same way that it did for my colleague.

Hand me a pair of secateurs or a trowel and let me loose in the garden, however, and it is a different story. All I can think about when I have a trowel in my hand is weed this, move that, cut back those, prune this. I move from one task to another, often getting distracted halfway through one area in the garden to work on another. I frequently lose my tools, since I put them down while doing one task and move on to another part of the garden without thinking. And, boy, does it do me good! Whenever I am feeling a bit stressed, even half an hour in the garden will completely change how I am feeling. It also makes me feel a bit better about losing my tools now I know why I am so prone to doing this!

For many, their right-brain activity will be exercise, such as running, cycling or swimming, or a team sport. Calming the brain certainly doesn't have to involve calming the body! The UK's Victorian Prime Minister, William Gladstone, famously used to resolve much of his own anxiety (of which he had more than his fair share) by cutting down trees; people used to send him axes from all over the world for the purpose, which was good for him, but not so good for the trees! For others, music can be a great way to tap into the right side of the brain, either listening to it or playing it themselves.

Creative activity often allows our brain to rest in this way, which includes art, but also simple colouring, sewing, knitting, woodwork, baking, cooking and more. The more the activity is for its own sake rather than because it must be done, the more relaxing it will be. Once there is a deadline and pressure to make something, then the soothing effect of the activity will diminish, and for some, especially those whose paid work is highly task-based, their best activity will not involve achieving or creating anything. Learning the skill of simply sitting in the garden and watching the birds can be enormously therapeutic.

Ultimately, you can ask yourself what activities lead you to feeling deeply absorbed and lost in them, and which activities leave you feeling better, calmer and more whole after you have done them?

Left-sided distraction

Sometimes, when we are overthinking and get stuck in a rut of worry, we need to find something that distracts us but we might not be feeling creative! What are we to do then? There is certainly a place for distracting the left side of our brain – which we might think of when we play a computer game, for instance, or do a word puzzle, or scroll through social media. Without a doubt, these can all bring helpful relief from our worries, since these activities will often be very easy to engage in and require little effort on our part; they tend to appeal to the quicker left side of our brain.

The key thing to think about, however, is how you feel after engaging in left-sided distraction. If the effect is to leave you more relaxed and able to move on from your worries, then this may be a helpful part of your self-care. If, however, it leaves you feeling more wound up and tense, or if your worries flood back the minute you stop distracting yourself, then there may be better activities for you. I will go into more detail on this in Chapter 15, which is all about sleep.

Using right-brain activities to destress

If we are going to use right-brain activities to help us destress when we are feeling overwhelmed, we also need a range of these activities to suit a range of situations. Gardening may well be one of my favoured go-to activities to relieve stress, but it is not that helpful when it is raining or pitch-black outside. I may enjoy painting and know how much it calms my mood, but I need enough time to make it worthwhile getting my paintbrushes out, and it's not something I want to do in the middle of the night when I am struggling to sleep. We need to develop a range of activities, therefore, that suit us and work in different situations. Some will involve physical exercise, others will be part of our regular routine, some will fill an afternoon while others will be needed when we only have five minutes, or in the night when we need to turn our brain off and get back to sleep.

Using right-brain activities for sustainability

I often talk to my patients about the need to make sure their life stresses are sustainable. We can deal with stress, a lot of it; more often than not, we actually thrive on it. Many times, we can't avoid it, but we need to make sure it is sustainable or else we will burn out. Making sure there is regular time in your week for right-brain activities is one way of doing this.

If I look at my own working week, I work three long clinical days in my practice. They are intense, 12-hour days, with lunch snatched at the computer, and every minute feels precious. Sometimes I feel overwhelmed by it. And yet my week is sustainable because I have weekends and two days in the week when I am not in the practice. Often, I will have to log in from home to clear some of the admin tasks that are part of being a GP these days, but for the most part, this time away from the practice allows me to decompress my week and make it sustainable. I might do other work, such as writing or teaching, but I might also simply spend time in the garden, go for a walk or do some woodwork. If I didn't have this rhythm in my week – for instance, if I tried to work four or even five clinical days – I doubt I would last six months.

Making the week sustainable is key to avoiding burnout, but learning to value right-brain activities sufficiently in order to ensure we actually do them is more challenging. Often, they can seem to us to be non-productive, self-indulgent or just not urgent enough to demand our attention. The urgent/important grid can be helpful in our thinking here:

Urgent versus important

It can help to classify everything into how important they are to us and how urgent they are. It's vital not to confuse urgency with importance when we do this. Urgency simply means what sort of timeline it is on – in other words, whether it needs our attention now or can wait – whereas importance is a measure of how much we truly value something. We can then think about each of the four sections and how to manage each section.

Let's look at these in a bit of detail:

	Urgent	Non-urgent
Important	Will take care of themselves	Needs special attention
Not important	It helps to get rid of these	Time to declutter

Urgent and important
If something is both urgent and important it will grab our attention, and we will be happy for it to do so. We don't need to make sure it gets our attention and so we don't need to spend any energy focusing on this category, since it will take care of itself. An example for me at work would be a highly abnormal blood test that gets phoned through from the lab. It is urgent that I act on it now, since the patient could come to harm if I delay acting on it, but it is important enough that I am happy for it to interrupt what I am doing.

Urgent and unimportant
This category needs reducing as much as possible. These tasks are urgent, since they have to be done now, but they are not important to us. The best example of an urgent but unimportant task I was faced with occurred when I first started working in my practice.

It was customary at that time for all GPs to have a regular weekly meeting with a drug company representative, and it always became urgent on a Friday lunchtime: the drug rep was in the waiting room ready to see me, but it was never important! I placed no value on seeing them and simply continued for as long as I did because I felt I ought to, since the other doctors were doing it too. It took a while before we all worked out that it was not important and we had better things to do with our time (not to mention the ethical dilemmas of being influenced by Big Pharma!). Now I meet with my colleagues over lunch on a Friday; we enjoy a break in our day, check up on each other and talk about the weekend – an activity that is far more valued by us all!

Non-urgent but important
This is the category that needs special care and attention and is where all the right-brain activities lie. Whether it is exercise, art, going for a walk or sitting watching the birds, it rarely gets to the urgent category, since it can always be delayed or deferred. These are the things we always mean to do, want to do and know will do us good, but we never get around to them, or not as often as we would like. Quality time with family and friends is also in this category, as is learning new hobbies or writing that novel we always knew we had in us. We need to remind ourselves of just how important these activities are to us and give them sufficient value, so that we make sure they don't get pushed out. Sometimes timetabling these activities can really help – when the allocated time comes, they become urgent and so actually get done. This is one reason why it is much easier to take part in group activities like a team sport or an art class, since they get put in the diary.

Not urgent and not important
These items rarely push out more important things, but they can

add to unnecessary clutter. They are like the junk mail in our lives, the things we don't value but we sometimes waste time doing or thinking about doing. They are emails that we find ourselves reading when we should have just hit the delete button, the time we waste on social media or checking the news for the umpteenth time every day. We will be able to function perfectly well even if we don't deal with this section, but if we can learn to hit the delete button more quickly and put our phone a little further out of reach, then our lives will be less cluttered, and we will have more time for those non-urgent but important activities that really do us good.

In these last three chapters, we have considered who it is that gets burnout as well as how to approach recovery, but, of course, it would be better if we never burnt out in the first place! How to prevent burnout is a really important area for us to consider and is the subject of the next chapter.

Chapter 11

I don't want to get burnout

How do I prevent it?

They say that prevention is better than cure. You may be surprised to hear that, as a GP, this statement often worries me. It is frequently quoted as a self-obvious mantra that must always be true, but this is not always the case. To take a silly example, for instance, you could prevent virtually all prostate cancer by removing the prostates of all men before the age of 40, but the downsides of such a preventative approach are obvious! For other medical interventions, such as taking statin tablets to try to prevent heart attacks, for instance, the balance of benefits and harms is more nuanced, but almost nothing in medicine is completely harm-free, and that includes making changes to try to prevent burnout.

It may seem odd to start this chapter by talking about the potential harms of trying to prevent burnout – what could possibly be wrong with trying to do that? And, indeed, I don't think there are many harms, but I suspect people who are at risk of burnout have inhibitions, worries even, about what might happen if they do try to prevent it. You may have been so defined by your approach to work that you will worry about doing things differently.

Will I be the same person? Will I just become selfish if I try to look after myself more? Do I deserve to be happy? What will other people think of me if I change? These are just some of the questions you may be asking yourself – either consciously or unconsciously – when you think about preventing burnout. Do you want to prevent burnout? Of course you do! But you might worry about the cost of doing that, and I want to reassure you that you can absolutely prevent burnout without becoming a different person, without becoming selfish overnight and without letting people down. So how do we do this?

Keep some space on your hard drive

My own experience working as a GP is that I could very easily burn out with the stress of the job; there is no doubt that it is full-on when I am at work. It is both physically and emotionally demanding, and there are times at the end of the day when I feel totally exhausted. The closest I came to actual burnout was probably in the summer of 2018. I became increasingly aware of the signs of stress, and all too often there was a rising sense of panic when I looked at the week ahead and wondered how I would fit it all in. Weekends and evenings were often spent squeezing work and other commitments between eating and sleeping. I didn't burn out, but it certainly wasn't healthy.

At the time I was working three intense, 12–13-hour days in the practice and had a secondary role as a programme director for the Guildford GP training scheme, on top of which I was also part of the leadership of a local church. I had thoroughly enjoyed the training role over the previous ten years, but it was becoming increasingly burdensome, and the emails seemed endless. I had done quite a bit of medical writing by that time and knew it was something I found very stimulating, so when a job came up at the

British Medical Journal as a regular columnist, I decided to apply. In fact, I wasn't even shortlisted for the role, but it was a pivotal moment for me as it made me realize that my plate was too full and something needed to change.

I wanted to write more, but I needed to make space for it, and so I resigned from my training role, which left me with a whole day a week to write. It was bliss! I still had my intense clinical days, but every Thursday I would wave my wife off to work, turn on some music, get myself a mug of coffee and open my laptop, ready to spend the day writing. The altered rhythm in my working week, the sudden drop in the stream of emails and the complete sense of control I felt on my writing days all made a dramatic difference to my wellbeing. And 18 months later my first book, *The GP Consultation Reimagined: A Tale of Two Houses*, was published!

What I have discovered in finding this pattern to my week is the importance of making the week sustainable, and this means keeping some of my hard drive empty. Our computers have a memory bank on their hard drive, but whatever their capacity, we have all learned what happens when the hard drive fills up: the computer suddenly falls over and every minor task it performs seems to take an age. This is because when computers are doing their thing, they need to be able to pick up a piece of code, work with it and then put it down somewhere while they pick up the next piece. When the hard drive is full, the system finds it hard to put things down; it has to squeeze them into the final few megabytes left in its memory, and this takes so much longer than when it has plenty of room. Everything grinds to a halt as it takes so long to process even simple tasks.

A similar analogy is when you pack your car to go on holiday; if you have plenty of space in the boot and suddenly remember that you need the sun cream that you have already packed, it is no trouble to find. But if each bag and suitcase has been neatly

choreographed to fit into every available inch of space, then getting to the sun cream is much more challenging!

Whatever it looks like in our individual lives, we need to learn to value leaving some space on our personal hard drive. What might this look like? Well, it might involve a significant change to our circumstances, as it did for me in 2018, but it might just mean a tweak here or there. The first question to consider is how much space we might need. Computers operate very well at 70–80 per cent capacity and we are similar – we don't need to empty ourselves of stress and responsibility to be able to thrive. In fact, as we have seen in Chapter 9, some stress is good for us! What would 70–80 per cent look like for you?

If you are working, it might mean a change to your hours, or it might be that work would be okay if it were not for the many responsibilities you have outside of work. For some people, laying down just one burdensome responsibility can make a profound difference. For others, it may not be our working hours that need to change, but the way we work; perhaps we need to do things differently at work? Maybe we really do need to learn when to delegate or how to let go of some of our responsibilities.

Letting go

Letting go is not easy! Sometimes we hold on to responsibilities out of a feeling of guilt; we don't want to dump on others, since we assume they are as stressed as we feel. And yet if we hold on to everything until we break, that won't help anyone! By letting go of some of our burden, we may be better able to do the job that we are meant to be doing and actually lessen the burden on those around us. The amount a task stresses us varies from person to person, so a task you dread having to do may be no bother for someone else, while you could just as easily take a burden from them without it feeling heavy at all. We need to move beyond our initial feeling of guilt to look at which tasks we are responsible for and whether or not we are the best person to do them.

Sometimes we find it hard to let go because we don't trust that others will do the job as well as we do; we are tied to the old mantra that 'if you want a job doing well, do it yourself'. There is some truth in this, of course, and there is always a risk that if we let go of something, then it won't be done so well. But there is also the very real possibility that once we step back and give someone else the space, another person might grow into the role we have left behind and do the job just as well, or maybe even better. We may even be afraid to let go exactly because we worry that someone might indeed do it better! There is always a risk involved in letting go, but if we want to prevent burnout, then it is something we need to learn.

It doesn't have to be much

People will often say to me, 'But I can't stop doing anything!' I can imagine how this must feel. Maybe you are self-employed and finances are tight; if you cut back on work, then how will you pay your bills? Or you look after a child with complex needs, or elderly parents who are getting increasingly demanding, or both. Primarily, though, I think this is less a statement of incontrovertible fact and more a cry for help. This is how we feel when we are overwhelmed and panicked, when solutions are eluding us and problems are crowding in. It may be very hard to find anything that can change, but that doesn't mean it is impossible. The key thing to bear in mind is that it doesn't have to be much; sometimes just making one or two small changes can make a difference and you feel as though you can breathe again.

One way of thinking about it can be to turn the puzzle on its head: is there anything I could do that would make me closer to burnout? It will probably be easier to imagine this! You could agree to an extra piece of work, for instance, or pull your child out of nursery so that you have even less time to get through your week, or turn down that one offer of help from your parents' neighbour who has volunteered to do their shopping once a week. The mental trick with this is that if you can imagine things that could make it worse, then it becomes easier to imagine that something might make it better. The level of stress you are under is not a static, immovable object, but a fluctuating wave that you can influence. So, what one small thing could you do to make it just a little bit better?

Is there one small commitment that you could pull out of? Maybe you don't have to clean the house quite so often, or you could use a slow cooker so that dinner is ready when you get home, or perhaps your teenager could help out more, or your garden doesn't have to look quite so immaculate – let the grass grow for a few weeks. Maybe you could actually afford to turn down work occasionally so that you don't get overwhelmed. Only you will know the answer to what would be the right change; if there is one thing I have learned as a GP, it is that the solutions my patients come up with themselves are always better than anything I suggest! I may be able to nudge and guide them to the right area, but they know what will work for them better than I do.

Moral distress

Lastly, a topic we should talk more about is the role of moral distress in burnout. This is the psychological distress we can feel when we know the correct ethical action we should be taking, usually in our workplace, but we are unable to take this action due to the constraints that are placed upon us.

This is very common in health and social care, but it can occur in any workplace. It may be a doctor who knows the patient they are with really needs more of their time, but is too aware of all the other patients waiting to be seen to be able to give it to them. Or a carer who is under pressure to spend no more than 15 minutes in their client's house when they desperately need longer. Or a mental health practitioner who is compelled to reject perfectly reasonable referrals as the service is so overstretched, or receives the rejected referral for one of their patients and feels powerless to help them. Or a teacher who feels they are letting down the whole class because the needs of a few children are not being met. There are so many other examples, both in and outside the workplace.

Moral distress is common, and it amplifies the stress we are under like a multiplier, making the weight of our workload seem two or even four times as hard to bear. Moral injury is defined as when the distress caused leads to a significant impact on mental health – it is like an accelerator towards burnout. Preventing burnout is not simply a matter of reducing workload, but also considering the nature of that workload, and how in tune it is with our values. Work culture can be so important here. Working under pressure with limited resources can be sustainable when it is as part of a supportive, caring team, whereas working in a toxic, critical or uncaring environment can be very distressing and quickly lead to burnout. How to create a morally supportive work environment is a challenge for leaders, and well beyond the scope of this book, but we need to talk about moral distress, and minimizing its impact is an important part of preventing burnout.

What else can help?

So far, we have looked at how to understand anxiety and its important relationship with avoidance, as well as the need to look after ourselves and both manage and prevent burnout. In the final section of the book, we will now turn our attention towards how to plan a recovery. We will look at the importance of getting our sleep and our breathing right, and a process I call anxiety rehabilitation, before looking at specific treatments, including both therapy and medication.

Part 3

Managing anxiety, taking charge

Practical steps for making progress

Chapter 12

Anxiety rehabilitation

Planning your recovery

When an athlete is recovering from a serious injury, they will engage in a programme of rehab – or rehabilitation, to give it its proper name. Initially, this might simply involve rest, so that they don't make their injury worse. Subsequently, with the help of a physiotherapist, they will start on a recovery plan. Steps will be small at first – maybe a series of gentle exercises to get things moving or stop their muscles weakening through disuse. Gradually, they will increase these exercises as they rebuild their muscles and joints and get their body to perform once more. What's important is that the rehabilitation exercises are not the goal; they will probably be boring and repetitive, they may be painful and require a great deal of effort, but they undertake them in order to achieve their greater goal, which is to compete again.

Now, not many of us would class ourselves as an athlete (I certainly wouldn't!), but the principles of rehabilitation can apply to anyone who has been physically or mentally injured. On the physical front, I often encourage my older patients to use these principles when they are recovering from a fall, since older people are especially vulnerable to their muscles weakening rapidly once they stop moving. They laugh at the comparison with an Olympian, but those who get it recover more quickly and more thoroughly than those who don't. So, what about mental rehabilitation? Shouldn't we expect the same principles to apply?

Steps on the road to recovery

If we are going to think in terms of rehabilitation, then a key principle will be to expect some sort of planned, graded recovery. A sprinter doesn't go straight from the physiotherapist's couch to a 100-metre race, and nor should someone affected by anxiety just go out into the world regardless of their fear. So what might these steps look like?

Rest

The first question to ask is this – like the athlete, do you need a period of rest? It may be that your anxiety has become so overwhelming that you need to take actions that simply allow your mind and body to stop and breathe again, to be able to see the wood for the trees and get to a point where you can start to imagine recovery. It might be that you need to remove yourself from a pressure-cooker situation – do you need some time off work? Should you reduce your commitments, step back from something that is stressing you or just take action so that you can get a better night's sleep before you do anything else?

This may well be a time to go and see your GP, if you have not done so already. It can help to simply talk over the issues with them; they might give you good advice, but, more often in my experience, it is through the act of talking that you gain a different perspective and become better at understanding the right steps to take. It might be that you are so overwhelmed that this would be a good time to talk to your GP about medication (by which I mean the imperfectly named antidepressants – see Chapter 18 for a whole chapter on the role of medication), but medication may not have to be part of your recovery.

Rest is important, and it may take some time before you are ready to move on, but the athlete is not going to get back on the track if they rest forever, and so you will also need to move on to the next stage if you want to recover.

Stem the tide

Anxiety might be restricted to one contained area of our lives, but the vicious cycle of anxiety and avoidance can easily lead to an ever-increasing succession of situations that are drawn into its orbit. What was once just a fear of going to large parties led to avoiding crowded places, turning down opportunities to go to concerts or a football match, then avoiding big family gatherings and now making excuses for any social event other than with a few trusted friends.

Sometimes this happens slowly over a number of years, with each pattern of avoidance becoming normalized, and layers of avoidance being added so slowly that you have hardly noticed the change. Sometimes anxiety comes in a rush, seeming to arise out of nowhere and with the sequence of anxiety and avoidance being more like a twisting, whirling tornado that takes your life in its grip and won't let go. Either way, if left unchecked, the tendency is for anxiety to demand more over time, and the first step to rehabilitation is to halt its advance.

Take stock of what anxiety has not yet stopped you from doing and ensure that it stays that way. This is the equivalent of the athlete starting some simple exercises so that she doesn't lose her general fitness while she recovers; she is not yet building her fitness back up, she is simply making sure that she doesn't go backwards.

You might find it helpful to do a visual exercise to help you identify what areas of your life anxiety is currently affecting. Draw a circle in the middle of a large piece of paper, and then two concentric circles around it like this:

Figure 12.1: Comfort zone, expansion zone and no-go zone
Adapted from the comfort zone, stretch zone and panic zone concept
for learning and personal growth, origins unclear

You might want to use coloured pens so that you have a green, amber and red zone, but that all depends on how much you like coloured pens! Think of the innermost (green) zone as your comfort zone; this is where you can function freely, where anxiety might not be absent, but it doesn't stop you from operating. Start to write a few things down in this area, beginning with those things that are most familiar to you – perhaps your close family and friends, perhaps your home or areas close to your house, maybe activities that you enjoy and that don't cause you stress.

Don't try to think of everything at this stage; just get a few items down on the paper – you will see that you will need a large piece of paper and much larger circles than the ones above!

Next, start to add some things to the outer (red) zone. These are activities or situations that anxiety currently stops you from doing, but you would be happy to never do in your life. We all have something to put in this zone – the first one I always think of is bungee jumping! I know I would be far too terrified to bungee jump and, quite frankly, I never want that to change! What goes in this zone, however, is different for different people. For some, it might be performing on stage, while others love to be on a stage – or would love to be able to do it, if only they could overcome their anxiety. If it is something you would like to be able to do, then it doesn't go in the outer zone. The outer zone reminds us that anxiety is normal, and that it is okay to have some things that are not only in your 'no-go' zone but are in your 'never-go' zone.

The middle (amber) zone is for those activities or situations that your anxiety is currently preventing you from doing, but which you would ideally like to be able to do again, or maybe to do for the first time. We need to put things in this zone that are realistic goals; for instance, I might like to be a professional footballer, but that is too unrealistic to go on my page – it is not anxiety that prevents this, but talent and being far too old!

Having got some things down in each of the zones, keep thinking of areas of your life and put them into one of the three zones until you have filled each of the circles. Don't try to be too precise or worry too much about what goes where at this stage – you can always move things around later – but try to think broadly until you have run out of new items to add.

As you look at what you have put down, your focus at this stage in your rehabilitation will be to make sure that those items in the innermost zone remain exactly there and don't drift out of your comfort zone. By identifying them, you can pay them special attention so that you notice them, feel good about the fact that you can still do them despite your anxiety and become determined not to let go of them.

Dipping your imagination into the expansion zone

The middle (amber) zone is your expansion zone; it contains what you would like to be able to do, but currently your anxiety is preventing you from going there. It feels like it is a 'no-go' zone at the moment, but what would it feel like if you *could* start to do some of those things? Take one item in this area that is important to you and imagine how you would feel if you were able to overcome your fear and do it. What would that mean to you? Who would be the first to notice? What would they say? What would it be like if, in time, that item in your expansion zone were to be part of your comfort zone, meaning that your comfort zone had expanded to incorporate it and you were able to do it and, one day, even forget that you ever felt afraid of it?

The reason for thinking like this is that imagining change is the first step to bringing about change. It is like the athlete dreaming of finishing a race once more, or being on the podium and having a medal placed around their neck; that is the driver that gets them through the training. To make progress with anxiety, we need a driver as well. The sense of freedom, confidence and joy that overcoming anxiety can bring is a very powerful driver, and we need to imagine those emotions as part of our work towards achieving them.

Dipping your toe into the expansion zone

The next step is to plan your first exercises in your rehabilitation.

This is where you will start to grow, but it needs to be baby steps at first. Look at what is in your middle expansion zone and ask yourself which item you would like to tackle. It will help if it is an item that doesn't seem too difficult, but what is important is that it is one that matters to you right now. If it seems too daunting to even think about, your only task at this stage is to imagine the very smallest step that you could take towards achieving this goal. The smaller the step the better; if it is laughably, embarrassingly small, even better. The next step is to commit to a time and a place where you are going to do it.

Facing the shops

Adam found it difficult to leave the house; it had crept up on him over the last few years; he felt okay at home and anxious when he went out, so he stayed home. He could do some things – things he had to do, like go to work or visit his mum – but he always went by car; the roads were familiar and it helped that he knew the people he would meet when he got there. It was the unknown that bothered him, the not knowing who you might meet, what you might say; he had never been good socially. Going to the shops was something he had avoided for so long he had forgotten what they looked like.

Online shopping was just so convenient, he had a good routine with a weekly grocery delivery, and with Uber Eats he could even order items he had forgotten, or run out of, and they would be there in a jiffy. You didn't even have to talk to anyone on the phone.

Deep down, though, Adam knew that it wasn't right that a trip to his local corner shop was out of bounds. His son was getting older and starting to ask questions; how was a boy meant to learn how to grow up in the world when his dad couldn't walk to the shops? And, deep down, Adam was angry with himself that he hadn't been able to overcome this. Urgent deliveries were all very well, but it would feel good to be able to walk to the shop and get your own bottle of milk when you needed it. He just needed to know how to get there.

Let's take the example of Adam and think what might be a laughably small step for him. There is no doubt that just walking down to the local shop does not seem laughably small to him at all – it seems impossibly large and insurmountable, and he doesn't know where to start. We can break down his task into a series of steps like this:

1. Put coat and shoes on.
2. Go out the front door.
3. Go on to the street and walk down to the end of the road.
4. Go along the main road and stand opposite the shop.
5. Cross the road and look into the shop.
6. Go into the shop.
7. Walk around the shop, looking at items to buy.
8. Place item in the basket.
9. Go to the till and pay.
10. Leave the shop.
11. Walk home.

Having broken down the task into such small steps, Adam can now ask himself which is the first item that causes him to feel nervous. It might be item 1, but maybe he is okay about putting his coat on and going out of the door, since he does this to go to work, and it is at item 3, walking down the road, that he first feels anxiety rise in his throat. That, then, is where he should start.

And so Adam will commit to a time and a place to achieve item 3, to walk to the end of the road, *and then turn around and go home.*

The last bit is important, since the goal at this stage is not to go to the shop, but to go to the end of the road. This is something Adam will find challenging, but it is achievable; he is likely to succeed and can give himself a pat on the back when he gets home. He will have been anxious, but he will have managed his anxiety and pushed on nevertheless. The sense of achievement will make it easier to go and do it again, once more with the objective of simply going to the end of the road and coming home again. He continues to do this until it becomes normalized.

Maybe sometimes he meets someone in the street – he has to be ready for this and not run away when it happens. Perhaps he has thought of a strategy; a simple friendly hello and a smile can get you a long way. Meeting someone in the street then becomes less daunting – he managed it last time, surely he could manage it again? The street has become part of his comfort zone. The whole shopping trip remains in the expansion zone, but this part of the task has been overcome.

What is important is that Adam sees these trips to the end of the road as exercises; he is not doing them because he has run out of milk, he is doing them to weaken the power of anxiety and strengthen his power to overcome his anxiety. And so he doesn't wait for a reason to go to the shop or wait until he feels like going (more on feelings in the next chapter);

he goes because it is part of his training, and he makes it part of his regular routine.

With the street he lives on firmly in the comfort (green) zone, Adam now moves on to the next step – walking along the main road to the shop. Once more, he doesn't go in; he simply looks at it, notes that he has made the journey and heads home. Of course, Adam may feel that this is too slow, and if he wants to tackle several steps at once, then he can certainly do this, but what is important is that each new step feels achievable and that he can feel pleased with himself at having made it. If he can rattle through the steps quickly, then fantastic, but if he takes several weeks before he can finally purchase his first item, then that doesn't matter; what matters is that he is making progress, and progress that he hasn't made in years.

Of course, there are steps beyond going to the corner shop. The next goal might be going into the town centre, or meeting someone for coffee; it might be saying 'yes' to a work social having said 'no' every year for the last decade, or going to see the doctor, or picking up the phone. Once one item in the expansion zone has been moved to the comfort zone, then it becomes easier to tackle the next; the vicious cycle of anxiety and avoidance has turned into a virtuous cycle of overcoming and empowerment. This is why the middle (amber) zone is called the expansion zone, because your comfort zone can expand into it; there are no limits to how big your comfort zone can be.

Phobias

You can use exactly the same approach with the three zones when it comes to a phobia, but you will only put things related to the phobia in each of the zones. For instance, let's say you have arachnophobia, a fear of spiders, and you want to overcome it – what would you put in each zone? There would be items that you may be happy to put straight into the no-go (red) zone, such as owning a pet spider or holding a tarantula (although, interestingly, one person told me how, despite their life-controlling fear of spiders, they were not afraid of tarantulas, so this will be very personal to you).

Have a think about what you can put in the comfort (green) zone – it might actually be nothing at all, in which case I apologize as you are probably finding it hard to read this paragraph at all, but maybe you can start with the name 'spider' – are you okay to read it? To say it out loud? If so, you have something for the comfort zone. Then you can think about how you feel about very small spiders like a money spider, or seeing a dead spider, working your way up to what you can and can't do when you see a spider, or rooms you can't go into until someone has checked for spiders.

Just as for Adam, think of what your ultimate goal might be, and then break down the steps to get there in as small steps as you can imagine. Then take the very smallest step – maybe it is learning to say the name, or going into the garden in the autumn when there are more spider webs and looking at an empty web, or looking at pictures in a book. I can't tell you which is the smallest step as only you know your fear, but find a small step and go out of your way to practise it until it loses its power, then take the next step.

Psychologists call this exposure therapy, and it is powerfully effective for phobias. If you want evidence that exposure therapy works, consider what happens when someone with needle phobia develops diabetes that needs treatment with insulin. Studies have shown that about a quarter of the adult population in the UK have a degree of needle phobia, so that must mean that a quarter of adults who need insulin treatment have needle phobia at the time that they start treatment. Now I have met plenty of adults who are scared about the idea of insulin because of the needles, but I have never met a diabetic who needs insulin and remains needle-phobic. What does this mean? It means that phobias cannot survive regular exposure; the onslaught of exposure to a needle every day – maybe three or four times a day – is just too much for the phobia; it crumbles under such an assault and cannot be sustained. The need to inject so regularly normalizes the use of needles and the phobia is not only broken but crushed.

I can say the same for my own fear of dogs that I referred to in Chapter 3. As I grew up, I realized that if you want to leave your house, it is very difficult to avoid dogs; whether you are going for a walk in the town or the countryside, dog owners have this pesky habit of taking their dogs for a walk, and so you can't escape them! What is more, I also learned – to my cost – that running away from a dog is never a good strategy! And so, much against my instincts, I found that the best way to deal with the dogs I encountered was to stand very still and wait for them to pass. By having this enforced exposure therapy, with time, I learned that staying near the dog was not as scary as I thought and my fear receded. Now I can't claim to be a dog lover, but I am not afraid of them anymore.

Exposure therapy works – of this there is no doubt – but it is hard work. You might be able to do it on your own, or with the help of a friend, but you might also want to do it with the help of a psychologist, since the initial stages of exposure therapy will make you feel insecure, but it is important that you don't feel unsafe, since that can be traumatic. Learning how to control your anxiety while you are exposing yourself to your fears is key here; it is also important to consider how we imagine our anxiety, which is the subject of the next chapter.

Chapter 13

Dealing with the anxiety monster

Call him Wilbur and take him with you!

I've just been listening to a podcast where a woman called Emily described her experience with driving anxiety. It's a good listen if you want to check it out – it's from the 'A Healthy Push' podcast, episode 110. Emily describes having a panic attack when driving on the highway many years earlier; it seemed to come out of the blue, and her panic was compounded by the fact that the only way off this particular highway was on to another highway! She felt trapped and terrified, fearing she might pass out (she didn't mention her breathing, but I'm sure the dizziness she experienced will have been due to hyperventilation, which is why Chapter 16 is such an important chapter in this book). The experience was so profound that she has not driven on the highway in the 13 years since it happened, and for several years could not even be the passenger in a car unless they were driving on the back roads.

This pattern of avoidance persisted for a long time, and she learned to accept the limitations it placed on her, such as becoming increasingly dependent on her husband always being the driver, journeys taking longer, being unable to visit family like they used to. She tolerated this because the alternative of feeling that awful sense of panic again while in a car, and being unable to get out, was too overwhelming to consider. This went on until one day when she was invited to a family wedding. It was a three-day drive to get there, and highways were unavoidable, but she really wanted to go and had no option but to face her fear.

Sometimes, when we have been avoiding something for a long time, circumstances occur that make you contemplate doing that thing, facing whatever it is that has been terrifying you and you have hidden away from. It's a scary thought! It may be that, like Emily, there is something you want to do, or have to do, that is so important to you that you have to override your fear. It might be an exciting thing like a wedding as in Emily's example, or maybe you are given no option at short notice; perhaps your partner always does the school run because you get anxious at the school gate, but your partner is in bed with flu and there is no one else to call on at short notice; you are going to have to do it.

Or you arrive for a job interview only to find at the last moment that it is on the 25th floor; you always take the stairs as you feel panicky in lifts, but you can't arrive for the interview all hot and bothered after climbing 25 flights of stairs, and so the lift is your only option. Or perhaps, through reading this book even, you have decided to face your fears, break the cycle of avoidance and push yourself out of your comfort zone. But how do you do it? How do you face your fear without being compelled to run away again? Beth shared with me how this can feel.

Beth's story

My anxiety has become progressively worse over the past 25 years and I'm now borderline agoraphobic, so avoidance is very relevant.

I have a lovely, supportive GP and I have a pretty good

understanding of why and how this has happened (genetic predisposition plus cumulative life stressors), and I am fairly self-aware and emotionally literate.

However, understanding the why and the how doesn't always help in the moment when you feel paralysed by terror. Emotion tends to override logic in those situations.

Beth's experience, that emotion tends to override logic when you feel paralysed by terror, is something many people will be able to relate to. It's not that logic is of no use here, but emotions generate very powerful feelings that can easily overwhelm us, and, if you are facing your fears, it is likely to be this prospect that will most concern you.

Do it quickly and hope for the best!

This is one of the most natural approaches to take when we are faced with our fears. And for something like having to do the school run or being forced to go to the supermarket for that essential ingredient, it can be very appealing; gird your loins, dash in and out, hope anxiety doesn't have time to notice and maybe you'll get away with it this time! It might feel a bit like a trip down sniper alley, but it really can work...until it doesn't!

The biggest problem with basing our plan on the hope that we won't get anxious is that the entire strategy begins unravelling as soon as we *do* start to get anxious, and falls apart completely once panic sets in. This can then reinforce the strength of feeling in our minds that we were foolish to try, and that avoidance is by far the safer option; we have gone backwards! And even when it works, we are left with a feeling that we got away with it, which gives us no grounds for confidence the next time; you can't keep running the gauntlet of sniper alley and expect to never get shot, after all.

Introducing Wilbur

Beth is entirely right that sometimes logic is pushed aside by the overpowering nature of emotions, and so, while we should not abandon logic and should use the power of our mind to help us manage our emotions, it also makes sense that bringing counter-emotions to our aid could be helpful. The emotions of fear, dread and panic can seem dauntingly powerful, but we should not underestimate the value of more positive emotions like humour, silliness and playfulness. Fear might well up inside us like an uncontrollable force, but if you have ever tried to suppress smiling when someone is trying to make you giggle, or laughed so much that your sides hurt and you don't know how to stop, you will know the potential power of laughter to overcome your body just as completely as panic ever does. If we want to bring these emotions into play, it will help to consider how we see anxiety.

It's a good question to ask yourself if you are affected by anxiety – how do you see it? What do you imagine when you think about your anxiety? You may not have thought about it before, so you might want to take a moment to think about this before you read on. You might see your anxiety like a terrifying monster, ready to jump out at you at any moment, untamed, unpredictable and uncontrollable; or maybe you see it as an enemy to fight, something to do battle with; or perhaps you imagine anxiety like an overlord who must be obeyed, who tells you what you can and cannot do, what you have to do and what you must not do. All of these are common and reasonable ways of perceiving anxiety, and yet there are problems with each, which I will deal with in turn.

Anxiety as a ferocious, unpredictable monster
The problem with imagining your anxiety as a ferocious, unpredictable monster (whether this is a conscious feeling or not) is

that it leaves us in a very weak and vulnerable position. We are the archetypal maiden tied to a rock and left to appease the marauding dragon, or the children in *Jurassic Park* hiding in the kitchen while being hunted by a pack of velociraptors. This is an understandable way to feel, but it simply reinforces our sense of fear and helplessness in the face of our anxiety; anxiety is in control of us, when we want to be in control of it!

Anxiety as an enemy to fight

Perhaps, instead of being the helpless maiden on the rock, we should be St George on an armoured steed, ready to fight the dragon? Or Katniss Everdeen from *The Hunger Games*, armed with her bow, prepared to take out the enemy with a single shot? It is certainly less passive to imagine doing battle with this thing called anxiety and trying to overpower it. The language of battle is very common in narratives around health – you will often hear descriptions of someone battling with their cancer, for instance, but there are real problems with thinking about health in this way. One problem is that the emotions of anxiety are very arousing and stimulating, and so are the emotions of battle; we are trying to counter our flight mechanism with a fight mechanism! The end result can be even greater arousal, with all that comes with it – the racing heart, rapid breathing, feeling of dread and so on.

And what if we lose? You will often hear news reporters describe how some celebrity has 'lost their fight with cancer'; as an aside here, please never do this! If someone wants to describe their own cancer journey as a battle, then that is up to them, and some people do find it helpful, but so many people affected by cancer find it upsetting to hear cancer described in this way. No one loses their fight with cancer! Some people die from it, because that is what cancer can do, but to imply they lost suggests they were somehow too weak to overcome it, or weren't trying hard enough, or weren't skilled enough to win, which is clearly both nonsense and extremely unhelpful. It is the same with anxiety; if anxiety is difficult for you, you have not lost or been a failure, anxiety is just challenging to deal with, that's all!

Anxiety as an overlord

I think this is one of the most common ways of perceiving anxiety, even if we don't know it. Hints that this is how you might imagine your anxiety are if you find yourself using language like 'I can't' or 'I have to'. Language like this implies that there is some external law, or force, that has dictated to you what you can and cannot do; it is given as an absolute, like a decree from a ruler who must be obeyed. This is understandable, since anxiety can seem exactly like this as it behaves in a powerful and over-controlling way, but it leaves us entirely passive. Maybe we are not as scared in a con-stantly-looking-over-our-shoulder type of way as if we imagined anxiety like a monster, or as aroused as if we were in a perpetual fight. We might even feel quite safe and comfortable, but only as long as we stay within the rules. As long as we remain an obedient citizen in the regime of anxiety, we are okay, and we come to be-lieve that we have no choice in the matter. It becomes so normal to be trapped in this way that we have forgotten what freedom is like, and venturing outside the rules becomes unimaginable.

Imagining a different way – Wilbur and the power of silliness

When we decide to push out of our comfort zone, either because we are choosing to do so in order to make some progress with managing anxiety or because circumstances have forced us to do it, the first and most important thing is to recognize that anxiety will be coming with us. We might not like it, but pretending it isn't there and hoping for the best won't help us, as it simply leaves us vulnerable to it jumping out at the most inconvenient moment and surprising us. So, take it with you, acknowledge its presence and even welcome it. Now think about how you would like to imagine your anxiety, and where exactly it might be when you go out.

In my household, we have a saying that if you can be silly before seven, then that's a good way to start the day! This is for workdays mostly, as sometimes being asleep before seven is also a good start to the day at the weekends! We have around half an hour to say something silly, walk in a funny way or do something daft. There's no pressure to do this (that would be stressful and defeat the whole point), but when we catch ourselves being silly in the morning, we will say, 'Silly before seven, it's a good start to the day.' Even saying that is a bit silly!

There is such power in silliness. I am not alone in this; I was first inspired to think about how important being silly was by listening to Michael Palin of Monty Python fame, who helped turn silliness into an art form. Being silly isn't difficult – you don't have to be witty, clever or good at cracking jokes, but you do have to be in an environment you can trust. You need to know that you are not going to be ridiculed, because we make ourselves vulnerable when we are silly; if you are worried about that, then try being silly when you are on your own or when you talk to the cat!

Why silliness? Its great strength is that it stops us from taking ourselves too seriously, while bringing with it light-heartedness and all the positive emotions that come with that. Anxiety, on the other hand, wants us to take everything very seriously. It sees threat and danger around every corner and tries to persuade us that we must be serious in order to deal with the danger, and it comes with all the heaviness of heart and negative emotions we are all too familiar with. Yet anxiety's desire for us to be serious is usually misplaced; the threat is only real in so far as there is the risk of being afraid and so it tricks us into being serious about anxiety itself. There are times, of course, when we must be serious, and a degree of anxiety helps us focus; Michael Palin recounts that he would prefer a brain surgeon puts silliness to one side while she is operating, for instance! But when we don't have to be serious, a bit of silliness can really help to change the mood that anxiety would want to impose on us. So why not introduce a bit of silliness to how you imagine your anxiety? And this is where Wilbur, the anxiety monster, comes in.

I have to apologize to anyone reading this book who is actually called Wilbur! I'm reliably informed by Google and my own experience that it is not a common name, and if you are blessed with such a unique name, I hope you can forgive me! I picked Wilbur just because it was so unusual, and since I don't know any Wilburs, my imagination is free to impose whatever characteristics I want on my imagined Wilbur, free from the influence of any real Wilburs in my life.

By imagining Wilbur as an 'anxiety monster', you can turn a potential unconscious picture of anxiety on its head, because the monster you are going to imagine is not a sinister, scary one, but a fluffy, slightly comical, bark-worse-than-its-bite type of monster. By objectifying anxiety in this way, you can start to change the associations you have with your anxiety. Instead of them all being frightening, you can start to bring new associations, where you have a little chuckle to yourself about your anxiety monster. The more you do this, the more your instinct will be to smile about your anxiety rather than cry. It won't happen overnight, but it can be a big step to reframing how you feel when you think of your anxiety.

The fact is, the more you can find your anxiety amusing, associate it with laughter, laugh (kindly) at yourself for some of the things it makes you do, see them as ridiculous in an amusing way rather than a foolish or cruel way, the better. So, make up a name for your anxiety – Wilbur is available if you want to use it, but you will probably find a better one yourself – and think about what it looks like. Is it a monster? Maybe it has inflatable horns that bend when you poke them, or no teeth and its dentures fall out when it tries to roar? What colour is it? Is it fluffy or smooth? What are you going to say to it? And where will it stay when it comes with you? In your pocket? Maybe in your bag? Imagine where it is and then you can check on it whenever you want to and ask it how it's doing. If all this sounds a bit daft, then great – it means you are getting the idea!

Maybe your anxiety isn't a monster, and you would like to imagine it as an over-excitable puppy that wants to keep you safe but can't stop barking at everything that moves, runs about a bit too much and chews the furniture! Or perhaps a daft cat that keeps jumping up on the surfaces but enjoys a good stroke and a cuddle now and then. It really doesn't matter, and the way you imagine it will be better than anything I can suggest, but try to let your creative juices flow and change the way you think about your anxiety. And then we will be in a better place to start training your anxiety, which will include giving it some boundaries.

A time for worry

Pets can be a great source of fun, pleasure, joy and comfort, but they can also bring you reasons to worry! Our cats have been great at providing all of these emotions, and one of them seems to specialize in causing the last on this list! She is the adventurous one who climbs on to the roofs of our neighbours' houses and in and out of upstairs windows, while her much more sedentary sister thinks jumping on to a window ledge is a major acrobatic achievement! One day, when they were not quite a year old, there was no sign of the adventurous one when we got home from work, she didn't turn up for her evening kibbles, and there was still no sign of her when we went to bed. When I woke in the night, she was still missing.

The middle of the night is a great time for worrying! Lying there awake, unable to sleep, our worries can crowd in and multiply, with nothing to distract us other than the frustration that we are not asleep. My mind started to worry; what if she didn't come home? Maybe she had got lost or trapped somewhere? Perhaps she had been hit by a car or had some other accident and was too injured to make it home? Would we see her again? How would her sister react to being on her own when they were such good company for each other? All these thoughts whirled around in my head, stopping me from sleeping.

What characterized this worry was that it achieved absolutely nothing. There was no action I could take at two in the morning that would change the situation – we had already gone outside to call for her and checked the garage and the shed to make sure she was not shut in, and I was hardly going to wake my neighbours at that hour to ask them to do the same.

Worry is often like that; sometimes it stimulates us to take an action that will help, but, more often than not, worrying at a particular time or place achieves nothing. Yet how do we stop it? Just telling myself not to worry about my cat was not going to work; I care too much about her for that. And so I set my worry a boundary. I told myself that I was allowed to worry, but not right now; I gave myself a time when I would permit the worry to return, which was when the alarm would go off in the morning. At that time, I would have full permission to worry as much as I liked, but worry would have to wait until then. And with the help of reading my book for a bit of distraction, my worry was content to abide by this boundary; I had envisaged taking it to the morning and telling it to stay, and it obeyed. Two hours later my worries abated entirely when I was woken up by our adventurous cat sitting on my head!

Setting boundaries like this can be very helpful for managing anxiety and are easier to implement once we have objectified our anxiety, so that we can imagine taking it to the boundary and telling it to stay there. We can defer the time when our anxiety is allowed to be present, as I did in the night, or set a time limit on how long it is allowed to be in our thoughts. It might be, for instance, that anxieties crowd in at the end of a working day as you relive what you did in the day, worrying about whether you did everything right, remembered everything and so on. Telling yourself not to worry at all doesn't work for you since these thoughts keep wanting to crowd in until you have paid them sufficient attention, but you could set a time limit on how long they can occupy your thoughts.

Perhaps you are allowed to worry about them on your drive home, but they have to stay in the car and not come indoors with you, or maybe you say they can stay with you until you have finished a cup of tea once you get home, or until you reach a certain point on your journey home. When the time is over, you can imagine yourself like the Queen in the Netflix series *The Crown*, pressing the bell that signals your audience with the Prime Minister is over and enjoying the sense of a doorman escorting your anxieties away for now; you are in charge, and you have better things to do than to listen to them for any longer!

In the next chapter we shall look at a range of other practical tips for dealing with anxiety as we complete this section on rehabilitating our anxiety.

Chapter 14

Rehab hints and tips

Something here for everyone

Doing rehab is hard, and just as there are hints and tips that can make physical recovery more successful, so there are some really helpful tips that will help you on your mental health recovery. Here is a smorgasbord of a few such tips; they are take-it-or-leave-it: some you will like and some you won't, but read them all and see which resonate with you.

Tip 1: Don't wait until you feel like it

One of the fundamental principles in mental health rehab is that it is dependent on action. Actions are a great way to deal with negative feelings (more on this in Chapter 17 which is all about cognitive behavioural therapy) and rehabilitation depends on taking actions. An athlete will never get back to running if they don't choose to go to the gym and train; in the same way, we won't make progress out of our comfort zone unless we start to push a little bit. If we want to make progress, then we have to act, but we will only very rarely *feel like* taking those actions. Not only will we have to contend with the challenge of whether or not we feel motivated, but our feelings *love* our comfort zone! It is all safe and cosy and where we feel best, so why would we ever *feel like* leaving it? And so, we have to plan to take the actions that we know will help. When it comes to planning rehab exercises, it might help to diarize it. When will you go? How often? How will you know when you have done it?

Tip 2: Use your motivation to create new habits

Motivation is a funny old thing! At times, it feels like it is sky high; you are absolutely determined to make a change in your life and to make it happen; it feels as though you are sure you will succeed, and nothing can stop you. Then you wake up the next day and the motivation seems to have vanished in a puff of smoke, because the natural tendency for motivation is to wane over time; it is like a slow puncture in a tyre – unless you keep pumping it up, it keeps going flat. And self-motivation is harder still.

In my student days, I had a brief spell as a rower. I wasn't very good at it and missed all the races at the end of term when I sprained my ankle an hour before the first race, but I did enjoy it at the time, despite the early mornings. On the whole, I don't mind getting up at a reasonable time, but needing to be by the river at 6 am was challenging, although it actually required very little motivation on my part – because I knew that if I didn't get up, then eight burly blokes (well, seven burly blokes and a rather small cox!) would turn up and tip me out of bed! The key thing is that the lack of choice made it easier to turn up on time. It is the same with going to work; I don't wake up on a Monday morning and ask myself if I feel like going – I just know that I have to go. Self-motivation is a whole lot harder. There are times when I have set myself the task of getting up really early for something like going on a run, or just to enjoy the peace of the start of the day thinking it would do me good. I have never lasted longer than a week! My motivation waned, I had set myself too high a goal, and my bed was too cosy to leave.

Motivation, therefore, is an important driver but a fickle master. Habits, on the other hand, are the exact opposite. Habits don't wane over time; they harden over time – we become used to them and feel uncomfortable if we don't do them. And I am not talking here about 'bad' habits, or addictions, but normal everyday activities that become habitual. A simple example is the order in which we get ready in the bathroom in the morning. My habit is to brush my teeth, shave and shower in that order. There is no harm doing it in a different order, but it feels very odd. It requires no motivation to shave in the morning, because it feels so odd if I get in the shower and have forgotten to do so.

And so the trick is to use our motivation to change our habits, one small habit at a time. And the habit needs to be small – again, laughably small – so that it can be sustained for long enough to become a habit.

Here's an example from my own life. At my practice, we always have a coffee break at 11 am. All the doctors have a break in their surgery, and we spend a few valuable minutes refreshing and chatting over a coffee before we head back to work. For the first few years, I always had a couple of biscuits with my coffee, but there came a time when I thought I should eat more healthily and was motivated to make a change to my diet. I decided to change the biscuits for an apple. It was a small change and so, despite the disappointment I felt each morning when I bypassed the biscuit tin while clutching my healthy piece of fruit, I was able to sustain it. Within a surprisingly short period of time, this change had become a habit, and now my tastebuds are ready for an apple every morning with coffee, to such an extent that if I forget to bring one to work and am forced to seek out the biscuit tin, I am deeply disappointed at the substitution. Fascinatingly, if I am working from home, I still often want the biscuits! It is the association with coffee time at work that has become habituated with an apple.

If you are motivated to make a change, think of one small thing you can do, something you are confident you can achieve, focus on that and make it a new habit.

Tip 3: The confidence rating scale

Being motivated to make a change is one thing, but being confident that we can put that change into practice is quite another. Here's a good way to help you understand your confidence and to work with it. Start by asking yourself, on a scale of 0–10, how confident you are that you can achieve the change you want to make; when thinking about rehab as in Chapter 12, this may be the first step of bringing something from your expansion (amber) zone into your comfort (green) zone. If 0 means no chance at all and 10 means it's already a forgone conclusion that you will succeed, what score would you give yourself? Let's say you score yourself a 4. Next, ask yourself: why am I not a 2?

It really doesn't matter what score you give yourself; the key thing is that you don't pass any judgement on the score (no bemoaning how bad you are for only giving yourself a 4!), but that you ask why you are not one or two points *lower* than you have scored yourself – because to answer that question, you have to start thinking about what gives you confidence, and this in itself can help to build your confidence. Maybe you have some confidence because you have made some changes already; maybe it is because you know you can be stubborn if you need to be, and you can use this stubbornness to your advantage; maybe it is because you have broken down the challenge to such small steps and so this has helped you to believe you can start. Spend a bit of time thinking about what gives you confidence to achieve this specific goal – try not to rush this.

The last step is to ask yourself what could make you one more than you originally scored; say you scored a 6 – what could make you a 7? It might be that you set an exact date and time to start, and this boosts your confidence, or you break the task down into even smaller steps, or you enlist help from someone you trust. It might even be that just doing this process in itself has already boosted you to a 7!

Tip 4: Change your language

When we are feeling down or anxious, it is very easy to find ourselves talking in absolute, negative language. Words like 'can't' and 'don't' tend to dominate:

- 'I can't go to the supermarket.'
- 'I can't do needles.'
- 'I don't have the willpower for that.'

The problem with this kind of language is that it shuts down our thinking and our beliefs. It's very hard to work with a word like 'can't'; it doesn't leave any wriggle room for change. If you can't do something, then you can't do it, so there is no point in thinking about it.

Changing your language doesn't mean deceiving yourself; it is not about changing 'can't' into 'can' in one simple trick. It is all about adding some wriggle room to your thinking. Adding one simple word is a great start – the word 'yet'.

- 'I can't face the shops yet'

is a world apart from:

- 'I can't face the shops.'

There is room for manoeuvre when you use the word 'yet'. It is an acknowledgement that the situation *can* change, which opens the door to *imagining* change, which is always the first step to *bringing about* change.

A second word to introduce to your language is the word 'difficult' – how do these statements compare with the ones above?

- 'I find it difficult to go to the supermarket.'
- 'I find needles difficult.'
- 'I find willpower difficult.'

The power of the word 'difficult' is that it doesn't deny your struggles, or tell you to pretend you don't get anxious, or blame you for not finding it easy, but it does leave room for the possibility of doing the thing you find difficult, and raises the possibility that there may be a route to finding it less difficult.

Tip 5: Pace yourself

If someone is recovering from a physical illness or injury, pacing is crucial to their recovery. They don't do their exercises all the time or they would just exhaust themselves! And so it is with mental health recovery. While exercises and effort are important in making progress with mental health, so is rest and recovery. We need time when we are allowed to stay well within our comfort zone, so that it isn't hard work all the time; we need to practise things that help our wellbeing – like physical exercise, reading, creative space, time with friends and family. These should be things that are not hard work and that we know do us good. They are as important as the harder work of things like therapy and mental health recovery, and it really helps if we value them.

Tip 6: Turn a vicious cycle into a virtuous one

Vicious cycles are tough, and mental health is full of them! Whether it is avoidance fuelling anxiety; negative thoughts making us feel bad about ourselves, leading to more negative thoughts; or insomnia making us dread going to bed, so we are more likely to be stressed in bed and so less likely to sleep – there are many examples of how things can spiral downwards.

However, here is one undeniable truth about every single vicious cycle: no matter how vicious or how insoluble it seems, or how difficult it may be to imagine ever being free of it, wherever there is a vicious cycle, there *has*

to be a virtuous one – all you need to do is turn it around! If we stop to think about it, if doing one thing makes our situation a bit worse, then stopping doing that thing must help to slow the vicious cycle, and doing the opposite will make it a little bit better, making it easier to keep doing the opposite – we have found a virtuous cycle just by reversing the process.

So, if, for example, we are affected by insomnia and the dread of going to bed makes us anxious and so less able to sleep, one small change that helps our sleep will also have a small impact on how we feel about going to bed; this reduction in anxiety makes us more likely to sleep a little better when we do go to bed, thereby reducing our dread of bedtime and increasing our likelihood of getting better sleep!

Virtuous cycles are just as powerful as vicious ones; we just tend not to notice them as much since we are usually too busy enjoying the benefits of feeling better to scrutinize the process! It is easy to doubt this power, though, when you are going downwards in the spiral. Thankfully, you don't have to see the whole process in order to turn it around. Just ask yourself what one small step you could make that might be beneficial. What could you do that might help even a tiny bit? Or stop doing that is unhelpful? If you can start finding those small first steps, then you can see where it takes you.

Tip 7: Don't be like a politician

Winston Churchill once said: 'Democracy is the worst form of government – except for all the others that have been tried.' Now, he may have been feeling jaded when he said this, since he had just been ejected from office at the ballot box, despite successfully steering the country through the Second World War, but I have often reflected on the truth behind his statement. It is hard to think of a better form of government than democracy, but it is not without its faults, and one of its biggest downfalls is that it encourages our politicians to always think of their political future. There is no place for short-term pain for long-term gain, since the electorate will vote you out at the next election if you hurt them too much.

For this reason, the government of the day always acts for the short term while long-term, difficult decisions, like tackling the crisis of social care, lack of affordable housing or climate change, get pushed down the road for the next government to deal with. Short-termism is not the best way to run a country, and neither is it the best way to live a life.

Anxiety loves short-term comfort and makes us want to run away from anything that might expose us to those awful, anxious feelings. It has no sense of the future and is heightened to the immediate avoidance of threat and danger, which is what makes many of the solutions in this book quite challenging to contemplate. Your anxious brain will have read sections of what I have written and been shouting alarm bells in your head: Don't do it! You couldn't do that! Why would you want to? But you love feeling safe! And so on. If your brain has been trying to warn you like this, that is understandable, but you don't have to listen. And if you are sometimes frustrated by politicians who only think of the next election and never for the long-term good of the country, then maybe you can give your short-term anxious brain a bit of a talking to and say to it: 'I don't want to be like *them*!'

Tip 8: Look after your body – exercise, diet, caffeine and alcohol

The mantra 'a healthy body, a healthy mind' apparently dates back to a second-century Roman poet called Juvenal. I guess it has become something of a cliché, but a cliché that has been around for that long probably has some truth in it! It is to be expected that what we put into our body, and how we look after it, will affect our mental wellbeing, but it is easy to neglect this part of looking after our mental health. Taking exercise can help in the immediate term to deal with the feelings of anxiety, but taking enough exercise to feel physically fit can also bring a long-term feeling of wellbeing. In a similar way, we don't need complex scientific research to know that when we eat too much junk food, we don't feel physically at our best, which will never be helpful for our mental health.

Caffeine deserves special thought, since it will usually exacerbate our sense of anxiety due to it being a stimulant. Too much caffeine will make us feel jittery and shaky, and stimulate our bladder and bowels – all of which will be very familiar to anyone affected by anxiety. And that is before we get to its effects on sleep. We all know that a coffee before bed is never a good idea, but even a coffee at lunchtime can have an impact on the quality of our sleep. This is because the half-life of caffeine is six hours, meaning that it takes six hours for our body to remove half the caffeine from our system. One coffee six hours before bed, therefore, will leave us with the same amount of caffeine in our system when we try to sleep as half a cup of coffee just before bed. It's worth a thought!

Probably the biggest impact on our mental health, however, is the effect of alcohol. The recommended weekly safe level of alcohol consumption of 14 units of alcohol per week (about one and a half bottles of wine) is largely based on the risk of long-term physical damage from alcohol, such as liver damage, alcohol dependence or stomach ulcers.

The impact on our mental health, however, can also be short-term. Assuming you are not drinking dangerous amounts of alcohol, the question to ask yourself is what impact alcohol has on your mental health, and especially on your sleep. You may feel more relaxed when you have a drink, but does that have an impact the next day? Or the week overall? And what is its impact on the quality of your sleep? I don't believe that people affected by anxiety should have to be alcohol-free, but it is good to ask ourselves some honest questions about how alcohol affects us personally.

Pay attention to how you sleep and how you breathe

These two subjects are so important that they each deserve their own chapter, which will start the final section of the book.

Part 4

How else do we fix this thing?

Sleep, breathing and treatments

Chapter 15

Sleep

*How can we get so bad at something
we spend a third of our lives doing?*

Sleep is a great mystery. How is it that we can lie in one place, for hours at a time, oblivious to the world around us? What is our brain doing all that time? How do dreams work? What is their purpose? Why do we dream at all? How do we actually make the transition from wakefulness to sleep? And, perhaps most importantly of all, when we spend a third of our lives doing something, how can so many of us be so bad at it?

Of course, scientists do know a lot about sleep, even if they haven't unlocked all of its mysteries, but what matters most to the rest of us is how good it is to sleep well, and how rough it can be when we sleep badly. Poor sleep has a bad impact on mental health – we are more irritable and our mood is lower and our anxiety higher – yet anxiety is the great robber of sleep and so the vicious cycle just repeats. And once we start sleeping badly, it is so easy to get into bad habits that reinforce the problem; as with so many areas of our lives, the solutions that we fall into are often natural, obvious and totally the wrong approach!

I have many conversations about sleep with my patients. Usually, they start with a request for medication to help with sleep; not, I suspect, because people are desperate to take tablets, but because it is the obvious reason why you might see a doctor. We prescribe stuff, so it's the natural thing to ask us about; maybe it would seem odd to see a doctor about sleep if you didn't want to ask about medication? People are often surprised by what might be appropriate to talk to a doctor about; perhaps just getting advice about sleep doesn't seem a legitimate enough reason to book an appointment? I will talk about sleeping tablets in Chapter 18, but suffice to say here that the role of tablets to make us sleep should be minimal.

Marginal gains and sleep

When people have had sleep problems for a long time, they will usually have tried all the usual cures. Hot chocolate, a warm bath, reading a book, cutting out caffeine – they will have tried them all and failed at every turn. It is very easy to fall into the trap of trying them all in sequence, ticking them off each time they disappoint – 'tried that, didn't work' every time – before moving on to the next idea.

Good sleep can be such a difficult goal to aim for, such a daunting prospect, that it is easy to give up before you get started. There is a concept I find useful here, which was developed in a totally different setting: the goal of achieving Olympic gold. The daunting prospect of success in a velodrome generated the fascinating concept of marginal gains in the British cycling team, and it is a tale worth telling, since it may have something to tell us about how we could approach sleep.

When Sir David Brailsford became the head of British Cycling in 2002, he faced the challenge of trying to achieve success on the podium when the team had previously only won a single Olympic gold medal in the entire 76 years of its history. The gulf between where they were and where they wanted to be seemed huge, but Brailsford realized that rather than thinking big, he needed to think small. If they could make small gains, but repeat these gains in every aspect of cycling, then they could add together and make a real difference. Importantly, the small gains were goals that could be imagined and achieved.

They analysed every aspect of their sport, from the physiology, psychology and diet of the athletes to the dynamics of the bikes, the shape of the helmet and the nature of the training. They even thought about how to ensure good sleep for the athletes when away from home, including bringing their own pillows to use in hotel rooms. They called the theory 'marginal gains', on the basis that even a marginal gain, such as a 1 per cent improvement, was worth aiming for. Proving that any one of those marginal gains made a difference would have been impossible, since they were far too small to have an impact on their own, but the combined impact was enormous. In both the 2008 and 2012 Olympics, the team won seven out of the ten gold medals available in the sport.

When it comes to learning from the concept of marginal gains, we don't need to try to analyse our sleep with the precision that the cycling team used, but we can take on board its key principle: work on the small stuff, and don't throw out individual ideas because they don't work straight away. When it comes to the rest of this chapter, if you apply any one of the ideas and expect it to cure your insomnia, then you will be disappointed. On the other hand, if reading this helps you to think in a fresh way about sleep, if you make several small and achievable changes, and if your goal is not to achieve perfect sleep but to sleep better than you do now, then this will be a good chapter for you.

The importance of a good sleep pattern

The lure of the lie-in

Who doesn't love a lie-in? I certainly do, and just the bliss of knowing the alarm isn't set for the morning is often enough to ensure a lovely, relaxing night of sleep.

At least to start with.

For the weekend, it works fine, but holidays are different. Once I fall into the trap of letting the mornings slip from the usual 6.30 alarm, round to 7.00 and 7.30, I am getting into trouble. If I get round to waking up at 8.30, I am doomed for sure; the next night will be broken, and I can expect at least an hour or two lying awake in the night.

I should pick up the warning signs earlier, but I know the solution. The alarm has to go back on, even with a week of holiday still to go.

When a patient asks me for help with their sleep, the first questions I always ask them are what time they go to bed and what time they get up. What I really want to work out is which hours they are spending in bed, which of those are sleeping and which are spent lying awake. This is because I know how often sleep patterns can slip, and nothing will work to help achieve better sleep until this is addressed.

What often happens is that someone becomes so tired, due to poor sleep, that they go to bed early. It makes sense; they are tired and falling asleep on the sofa – wouldn't it be better to go to bed? And so they head upstairs at 9 pm and are soon asleep. But then they wake around 2 am and the rest of the night is fitful, mostly lying awake watching the clock slowly find its laborious way through a long night, until they eventually fall asleep again at 6 am and sleep until 8. What has happened is that they have actually had seven hours' sleep – five before 2 am and two after 6 am, but they have been in bed for 11 hours and the night felt terrible. When this happens, it is worth asking two questions:

- Which is the bigger problem – only having seven hours' sleep or being awake for four hours in the night?
- Would you swap a night of seven hours' broken sleep out of 11 hours in the bed for a night of seven hours' continuous sleep?

Most people would agree that while they would like to be less tired, and so an extra hour of sleep would be great, it is the tossing and turning, the frustration of lying in bed wide awake and the worry in the middle of the night that you are going to be tired in the morning that is the worst side of insomnia, and they would bite my hand off if I could guarantee them seven hours of continuous sleep, free from periods of wakefulness. Of course, I can't guarantee this, but I can help them head towards it.

There are three problems with going to bed early and getting up late. The first, and most obvious one, is that the average amount of sleep we can expect as an adult is seven or eight hours, and if we spend 11 hours in bed, we are guaranteeing ourselves something unpleasant – which is to be awake for at least three to four of these hours. The second is that in order to prepare for a good night's sleep, we have to have been awake long enough in the day for our bodies to be ready to sleep. Usually, this means being awake for around 16 hours. If we wake up at 8 am, this means going to bed at midnight, not at 9 pm. The third problem lies in the associations our brain makes. The more our brain associates the bedroom, the bed, the pillows, the dark and everything that should be linked with sleep with actual sleep, the more our brain will automatically settle into sleep patterns in that environment.

By contrast, the more our brain associates this environment with lying awake, worrying, problem solving and thinking, the more it will enter active mode when our head is on the pillow. We are back to conditioning; we need to be conditioned to connect the bed with only two things: sleep and sex (and healthy sex, as it happens, is also good for sleep!).

A second pattern I see is when sleep is not broken but has become reversed, so that someone goes to bed at 4 or 5 am and sleeps in until midday or early afternoon. They are getting the right amount of sleep, just at the wrong time in the 24-hour clock. Usually, the constraints of school, college or work prevent this pattern from happening, but it is challenging for someone whose week lacks this formal structure, who can easily find that their sleep pattern slips round in this way.

Restoring your sleep pattern

Once someone has decided that their goal is to achieve seven hours of unbroken sleep, the next question I ask them is this: which seven hours would they like them to be? This is important, because if you want to aim for this target, then you have to set the alarm for seven hours after you turn the light off. So, if you plan to turn the light off at 10 pm, then you have to have an alarm set for 5 am! Or, if you want to set the alarm for 7 am, then you will have to stay awake until midnight.

Wait a minute! Haven't I said that the average amount of sleep is seven to eight hours? Couldn't I set the alarm for eight hours after I go to sleep? Yes, you could, but if you have insomnia, then you are not an average sleeper, and having the light out for eight hours will probably mean lying awake in the middle of the night once again. Currently, you may only be getting five to six hours, broken up through the night, and so hoping for eight solid hours is probably unrealistic. If seven hours is too short, then you will sleep well in those seven hours, and once that is going well, then you can extend your night, but it is better to start with something that is not unrealistic; in fact, you might even have to start with six hours.

The idea that restricting the number of hours spent in bed can help with insomnia is not just limited to people with abnormal sleep patterns. There is good evidence that sleep restriction is one of the most effective forms of treating insomnia.[8,9] Even if your sleep pattern is not disrupted, it can still help to reduce the hours in bed to six or seven hours, as it can be one of the most effective ways of restoring better-quality sleep. I often tell my patients that the first night they try it, they will want to curse me for suggesting it, because their body will still be in the pattern of waking in the night and yet they have to get up when the alarm goes off, no matter how little sleep they have had. And yet, even within a few nights, sleep will start to improve if they stick at it.

Sleep hygiene

The term 'sleep hygiene' is used to describe healthy habits that can help make good sleep more likely. It's not a term I am keen on; it sounds clinical and makes me think more of disinfectant than the cosiness of a bed! It was coined in the 19th century, and so I guess we have the Victorians to thank for it, and we are rather stuck with it now. The concept, however, does encourage the idea that there are some general principles to try to put in place for good sleep, rather than one quick fix, which brings us back to the idea of marginal gains. So, what might some of these marginal gains be? Some are obvious and others less so, but we will go through some of the most important ones.

Marginal gain 1: Have a stimulation curfew

If you spend the hour or two before bedtime engaging with the things that worry you, whether it is work, clearing your emails or scrolling through social media, these are the things that are likely to pop into your head when you wake in the night, and once they are there, they will keep you awake. Many of these are important and will need to be done, but try to make sure there is clear water between them and bedtime.

Marginal gain 2: Be careful of screens

Screens, whether the television, tablet or phone, can have a big impact on sleep. I am not an expert on the direct effects of blue light on our sleep patterns, but even if concerns about this are unfounded, it is obvious that screens can be highly stimulating. Some people can go straight from a fast-action computer game to deep sleep in a matter of moments, but they are not the people who might benefit from reading this chapter! For the rest of us, the visual memory of the game will last well beyond when our eyes are closed, and we will need time to wind down before we can sleep. Similarly, a high-tension drama on TV will take longer to get out of our system than a gentle programme like a gardening show, while the addictive nature of scrolling through social media can have a very harmful effect on sleep.

What really matters, if you have sleep problems, is to ask yourself what the effect of screens is on your sleep. Do they stop you from getting off to sleep? If you wake in the night, is the content of whatever you were watching what fills your wakeful mind? If you have a TV in your bedroom, ask yourself why. Is it helpful or is it just reinforcing the association between the bed and being awake?

If you are used to falling asleep with the TV on, then really, really ask yourself why!

Marginal gain 3: Think hard about where you charge your phone

I have lost count of the number of times I have seen someone posting on social media that yet again they cannot sleep. Usually, fellow insomniacs reply and so at least the suffering is shared, but I can't help thinking: what on earth are they all doing on their phones? Looking at your phone in the middle of the night has to be the very worst thing we can do to help with sleep. It is visually stimulating and causes our mind to flit from one thing to the next, rather than settle and find peace. And yet many of us charge our phones in our bedrooms. Perhaps it is because our phone doubles as an alarm clock, or we feel we need it near in case of emergencies, or maybe it is just force of habit. It is a bad idea. Even if we put it on airplane mode so that it doesn't suddenly light up in the dark, it will tempt us to look at it once we are awake. Just a quick check, we kid ourselves.

If at all possible, charge your phone in another room. Use an old phone without a SIM card for an alarm if you need one, or invest in an alarm clock, and remind yourself that we didn't used to worry about being quite so contactable at every hour of the day before the invention of the mobile phone.

Marginal gain 4: Keep to a simple bedtime routine

Our brains love routines, and getting used to following the same routine in the half hour before sleep can really help the brain to associate the routine with sleep. Simple bathroom rituals form an important part of this, but so can having a warm, milky drink or reading a book. Choose your book carefully. Too exciting and you might not be able to put it down, too dull and you might not be able to get through the first page. If it is work related, you might turn the light out with your brain engaged in problem solving.

The actual time you go to bed does not have to be the same, though. We need consistency with when we wake up, since it is lie-ins that are the entry drug for poor sleep patterns, but it is always better to go to bed when we are tired and ready for sleep than feel we must have the same bedtime, knowing we are not ready and that we will lie there, wide awake, for hours.

Marginal gain 5: Go from warm to cool

An important part of how our body prepares for sleep is a small drop in core body temperature, and it helps to facilitate this by going from warm to cool. This is why a warm bath can be helpful as part of a good sleep routine. Keeping your bedroom cool and well ventilated (have a window slightly open throughout the year) is another marginal gain.

Marginal gain 6: Think about what you eat and drink

I mentioned the impact of caffeine on sleep in the last chapter, and the problem that it hangs around in our system for so long, so making caffeine a morning-only thing can be a real help.

It is also important to make sure there is not too much food in the stomach when we lie down. Eating too much, too late, can cause discomfort when trying to sleep, and even heartburn that might wake us up. Many of us eat late and go from table to sofa to bed without moving too much in between, and so our meal has not progressed beyond the stomach before we lie down and hope to sleep.

The relationship between alcohol and sleep is complex, with the sedating nature of alcohol meaning it can send you off to sleep, but its hangover effect meaning you are more likely to wake in the night and fail to feel refreshed in the morning. I was particularly struck by the impact of alcohol on sleep when I wore a continuous glucose monitor for a period of two weeks. I was interested to experience something of what it was like for my patients with diabetes to monitor their blood sugar in this way and was truly shocked to see the effect on my sugar levels one night when I had a nightcap just before bed.

That evening, I had a single shot of amaretto just before going to bed. I had not had any alcohol earlier in the evening and had eaten normally. When I awoke in the morning, I checked my overnight sugars and found I had had two episodes in the night where my sugars dipped alarmingly. The first dip caused my blood sugar to go as low as 2, when below 4 is considered to be abnormally low. This is significant hypoglycaemia! My body would have been working hard in the night, releasing adrenaline to try to get my sugar levels back up to normal, and it is no surprise that my sleep that night was restless and disturbed by hot sweats! Nightcaps are not a common event in our house, and after receiving this feedback, they are not going to be happening again in a hurry!

The sugar in the amaretto may have also been playing a part in this nocturnal event, since the body can overcompensate and make too much insulin in response to something very sweet, which may then send sugar levels too low two to three hours later. For this and other reasons, it is well recognized that eating something with a high sugar content just before bed can also have a very disruptive effect on our sleep.

Figure 15.1: The impact of a single nightcap on my nocturnal sugar levels

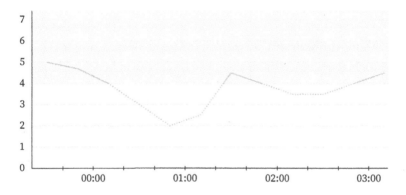

Marginal gain 7: Don't just lie there

It's important to have a strategy, or a range of strategies, for what to do when you are awake in the night. Once you have been awake for 10–15 minutes, if there is no sign of sleep, then it is best to do something rather than keep lying there, tossing and turning. Sometimes something as simple as going to the bathroom and back again will be enough, but other times you will need to do something to distract your mind and reset it for sleep. It may involve turning the light on and reading for 10–15 minutes, or going downstairs to read, or writing a list to store the things you have been worrying about so that they feel secure enough to forget for now. It might be lying in the dark but with a thought strategy that helps your mind turn off, like recalling all the steps of a familiar walk, tensing and relaxing all your muscles in turn or doing a spot of mindfulness. Be careful not to do something work related or visually stimulating; it can be very tempting to conclude that as you are awake, you might as well make use of the time, and you could use the time to answer a few emails, but you will be guaranteeing a long time awake if you take this approach.

In summary

The most important principles for good sleep are to work out which hours you want to sleep and limit time in bed outside these hours, and then to work on all the small steps that can help make good sleep more likely to happen. Don't expect results overnight, but also don't be resigned that, after years of insomnia, your sleep problems are incurable. You can sleep better, and that is worth aiming for, so keep an open mind and learn about sleep and what works and what doesn't. Consider cognitive behavioural therapy (see Chapter 17) for sleep, as it is one of the treatments that has the best evidence to show it works. And remember this: just because you have been sleeping all your life doesn't mean you actually know how to do it well!

Chapter 16

Breathing

*How can we get so bad at something
we spend all our lives doing?*

Breathlessness is always a serious symptom that I would want to assess in a face-to-face appointment, listening carefully to the patient's story and with a full examination. As a GP, I am in the privileged position of seeing patients who are breathless due to problems with their heart or lungs, as well as breathing problems related to anxiety. As with most aspects of medicine, you start to notice patterns.

When someone has a heart or lung condition, their breathing usually gets worse with activity, and never improves on exertion; they often have much more difficulty breathing out than breathing in; they don't get tingling in their hands and feet, and don't tend to feel light-headed. They rarely describe a feeling of 'not being able to get enough air' or an urge to take a deep breath in. Their oxygen levels might be normal, but they could also be low at rest, and lower still after exertion. Examination findings might give a clue as to the cause of their breathing difficulties, such as hearing a wheeze or crackling sounds with a stethoscope, a heart murmur or other clinical signs.

Breathing difficulties associated with panic or anxiety are quite different. The feeling of not being able to take in a full lungful of air is often prominent, while breathing out is not such an issue; sighing is common and breathlessness is more noticeable at rest, usually going away completely on exertion or when focused on something away from breathing; tingling and light-headedness will often feature, and oxygen levels will be normal or even high, never dropping on exercise. Examination findings will be normal, but I will often notice someone sigh prominently during the consultation, breathe through their mouth rather than their nose and use their upper chest muscles to breathe, rather than relying mostly on their diaphragm.

These are the differences between a *breathing disorder*, where there is a disease of the heart or lungs, and *disordered breathing*, when the heart and lungs are both working perfectly well, but the pattern of breathing has become abnormal. As a constellation of features, these two patterns are not difficult to tell apart, but when you are the one experiencing the symptoms, they can feel very much the same and are equally frightening. Which is why understanding your breathing is so important if you are affected by anxiety.

Holding your breath and over-breathing

We all know that it is impossible to hold your breath for more than a minute or two. The drive to take a breath becomes too much and we have to gasp for air, but why is that? Contrary to what you might think, it is not, in fact, because we need to take in air – it is because we need to get rid of it. That is because the drive to breathe has nothing to do with oxygen and is all about carbon dioxide. When we hold our breath, our oxygen levels will fall a little, but because we have a lot of oxygen in our blood and store it so effectively in the haemoglobin in our red blood cells, it would take too long for the brain to detect a significant change if there was a problem; and so the body uses carbon dioxide levels instead to know when to take a breath. The level of carbon dioxide in our blood is much lower than the level of oxygen, and so a small absolute change in carbon dioxide creates a significant percentage change, which is easy for our body to detect.

When we either hold our breath or exert ourselves (since our muscles use up oxygen and produce carbon dioxide when they work), the carbon dioxide level in our blood rises, and this stimulates the breathing centre in our brain and makes us take a breath, or breathe more quickly, getting rid of the carbon dioxide as we do so. This means that carbon dioxide levels are largely held very constant, even when we take vigorous exercise, and also in most people with a lung or heart condition. With some very longstanding lung conditions, or in someone in severe respiratory failure, carbon dioxide levels will rise, but otherwise levels will be neither too high nor too low.

Let's consider now what happens, though, if someone with a healthy heart and lungs starts to breathe faster than they need to. While there are limits on how much we can hold our breath, there is nothing to stop us from breathing too quickly; our unconscious breathing mechanism can easily be overridden, and this will cause oxygen levels to rise and carbon dioxide levels to fall. The rise in oxygen levels is not a problem, since too much oxygen is never harmful, although when someone's oxygen saturations are 99–100 per cent, this is a good clue that they may be overbreathing, since normal is 95–98 per cent. The low carbon dioxide levels, however, can cause all sorts of unpleasant symptoms.

Carbon dioxide, dissolved in water, is a weak acid, and so when we blow out more of it than we should, it changes the acidity, or pH, of our blood. The more alkaline blood that results causes temporary malfunctions in the way our nerves and muscles work, resulting in tingling (usually of the peripheries, so affecting fingers, toes and sometimes the tip of the nose), light-headedness and, at its extreme, cramping of the muscles called tetany. None of this is serious and it will all disappear once breathing returns to normal, but it is unsettling and can increase anxiety, thereby increasing the tendency to over-breathe.

It is possible to reproduce all these symptoms by simply making yourself hyperventilate (and when I examine someone's lungs, I always have to be careful not to cause these symptoms when I ask them to take deep breaths!). If you decide to have a go at this, it would be a good idea to have someone with you, and to be sitting down – not that much harm can result, but it would be embarrassing if you felt faint enough to fall over!

Disordered breathing, or hyperventilation

Hyperventilation can have two forms: acute and chronic. These are confusing terms and I remember being baffled as a medical student by what my lecturers meant when they called something acute or chronic. I was almost disappointed when I finally worked out their very simple meanings: acute in medicine just means something that has come on recently, while chronic means something long-standing. Acute hyperventilation, therefore, comes on quickly and is the dramatic over-breathing that someone will experience when they are having a panic attack. It will be obvious that they are breathing rapidly, and symptoms of tingling and light-headedness will be prominent, along with all the other symptoms of panic discussed in previous chapters.

Chronic hyperventilation, however, is much more subtle and easy to miss. It can mean as little as taking 14 breaths on average per minute rather than the usual 12, or breathing more with the upper chest muscles than the diaphragm, but it can produce a whole range of challenging symptoms, and understanding how to manage it can make a huge difference to managing anxiety.

I have found hyperventilation to be quite a difficult term when it is chronic; it is often not obvious that someone is breathing quickly, and telling people they are hyperventilating seems to go contrary to what they are feeling. It also somehow implies they are choosing to over-breathe. Describing the pattern of breathing as being disordered is a much more helpful way of thinking about what is really happening here, but why does the pattern of breathing change like this?

Trying not to yawn

Several years ago, a patient of mine whom I'd known for a long time used to poke fun at me whenever she caught me yawning.

'You're yawning again!' she would say, with a mischievous smile on her face. 'Am I boring you?'

It was always well meant, and we would have a good laugh about it, but the trouble was, I couldn't help it! She had a serious lung condition and usually came to see me when her breathing was bad, which meant she was noticeably breathless when she was in my consulting room. It was often late morning as it took a lot of effort for her to get up and out of the house to come and see me, and so I was probably a bit tired after a long morning surgery, but the main reason I kept yawning was nothing to do with that, and it was certainly not because my good-humoured patient was boring!

The trouble was that seeing her struggling with her breathing made me unconsciously think about my own breathing; the more that happened, the more I felt a need to take in a larger breath than normal, and this is closely related to yawning. The more I thought about trying not to yawn, the more I would struggle to fight the impulse to yawn. And I'm sure I had become conditioned to associate yawning with this particular patient, because it kept happening when I saw her!

Have you ever tried suppressing a yawn? Your face contorts into all manner of strange shapes, giving the impression of someone caught in an awkward combination of concentration, confusion and constipation; it's not a good look! No wonder she found it amusing!

We are all familiar with the contagious nature of yawning; when we see someone else start to yawn, it gives us the urge to do the same. A similar phenomenon happens when you are with someone who is breathless. It makes you conscious of your own breathing and, as with me and my patient, makes you want to yawn or take in a bigger breath of air than usual. This is the sharp, sighing intake of breath someone with a disordered pattern to their breathing will often experience. It is frequently described as feeling that you can't quite get enough air in, as if you are trying to get to the top of a hill each time you breathe but keep falling just shy of the summit. In fact, anything that makes you aware of your breathing can have this effect, so you may even find that reading this chapter all about breathing gives you a similar sensation of breathlessness!

And what happens if that person in the room, whose breathlessness has invaded your subconscious mind and made you have the urge to breathe like this, is actually you? The truth is that we usually don't notice our own breathing; we just get on and do it quietly in the background, 12 times a minute, unnoticed, unthinking. It can be very uncomfortable to become aware of your breathing, and once you start to notice it, then you can get the urge to take in these bigger breaths, and so you notice your breathing more and a vicious cycle can develop. This is also a reason why some people who develop disordered breathing will also have an underlying lung condition. Asthma is the most common one I see in practice. Someone with mild asthma can easily find that their mild symptoms lead to an element of disordered breathing on top of their asthma, sometimes leading to overusing their reliever medication, and wondering why it doesn't seem to help as it should.

The mechanics of disordered breathing

What is key to understand about a disordered breathing pattern is how the mechanics of ventilating the lungs in a disordered way are very different to normal breathing, and how this leads to symptoms affecting the chest and shoulders. Normal breathing is highly efficient and almost entirely powered by the diaphragm. This is the strong, almost effortless muscle that sits below our lungs and acts like a pair of bellows, pushing down as it contracts to expand our lungs when we breathe in, and relaxing when we breathe out, so that our naturally elasticated lungs recoil, expelling air in the process.

This normal pattern of breathing operates effectively for day-to-day activities, but we have the equivalent of booster rockets in our shoulders and rib cage for when we need to exert ourselves and up the rate and depth of breathing. These booster rockets are in the form of the intercostal muscles, which lie between our ribs, and the accessory muscles in our shoulders. The rib muscles help to stretch out the rib cage while the shoulder muscles act to pull against the diaphragm. In combination, they are really good at helping us to expand our lungs to the maximum, which is what is needed for heavy exertion.

The problem is that when we perform the deep intake of breath that constitutes a sigh, and when we find ourselves trying to 'get over the hill' and take in a full breath of air, we also have to use

these accessory and intercostal muscles. Muscles that are used to only being brought into action when we are pushing ourselves are now working on a regular basis; they were not designed for this and aren't very good at it. We are overheating our booster rockets! Before long, they start to complain in the form of chest pains and neck and shoulder pain. These muscular chest pains are not usually severe, but there is nothing quite like chest pain to increase anxiety, and to make us aware of our breathing, and so another vicious cycle can easily take hold.

Disordered breathing, or chronic hyperventilation, is sometimes called hyperventilation syndrome because of the wide range of symptoms it can be associated with. I'm not sure how helpful the word 'syndrome' is; it always makes something sound more alarming, I think, but it is used in medicine when doctors want to name something that causes a wide range of symptoms rather than just affecting one part of the body, and disordered breathing can certainly cause a wide range of symptoms!

The symptoms that are commonly caused by disordered breathing are:

- breathlessness (obviously!)
- chest wall pains
- shoulder/neck pain
- tingling
- light-headedness.

As well as other features of anxiety:

- feeling anxious (again, obviously!)
- palpitations, clammy hands, tremor, sweating (due to the adrenaline associated with anxiety)
- bowel symptoms such as loose motions, bloating and bowel spasm
- poor sleep.

And some other symptoms directly related to the breathing problem are:

- sexual problems (sometimes the need to take a breath can be a problem when it comes to being able to kiss and can be very distracting and disruptive during sex)
- fatigue (the extra breathing, as well as anxiety itself can be very tiring).

How do I know if I have a disordered breathing pattern?

Ultimately, if you have problems with your breathing, then it would be best to see a doctor to rule out other causes and help understand the nature of your breathing. Quite often, however, someone who has a breathing disorder will see their doctor about any one of the other symptoms that can be a result of it, and it may take a while for you and your doctor to realize the effect that your disordered breathing might be having on how you feel.

It is well recognized that disordered breathing patterns are often missed and go undiagnosed, including, I am sure, by doctors like me who have an interest in respiratory problems. Medical training always has a bias towards hard, identifiable disease of the sort you can test in the laboratory or see under a microscope, and so a topic like breathing pattern disorders can easily become a poor relation. I have been to more lectures on lung disease than I can remember, but I don't ever recall being formally taught about disordered breathing. So don't be afraid to suggest it to your doctor, as you might have to work it out together. Here are some of the things you could consider if you are wondering if your breathing pattern might be an issue.

For starters, there is a formal symptom questionnaire you can complete called the Nijmegen questionnaire, which is easy to find online provided you can remember how to spell it! This has some validated research behind it, although it was intended to help evaluate the extent that hyperventilation might be affecting a person, rather than as a formal way of making a diagnosis. A score of over 23 out of 64 can suggest hyperventilation syndrome, but it doesn't prove or disprove the diagnosis on its own and should be correlated with an assessment by a doctor.

You can also get clues if you watch the pattern of your breathing, although the challenge here is that if you know you are looking at your breathing, then that in itself can affect how you breathe! One patient of mine recently had the ingenious idea of looking at video recordings of remote meetings she had taken part in. Many organizations record these as a form of record keeping, and she went back and observed her breathing in some recent meetings. The sighing and frequent need to take a deep breath in between normal breaths were all there to see. Failing this, you might ask other people who know you well if they have noticed you taking big breaths like this, or you might try to become more aware of it and spot yourself doing it. Ask yourself how you hold your shoulders. When people use their accessory muscles to breathe, they tend to hunch up their shoulders and carry a lot of tension in their neck. What happens to your breathing when you drop or relax your shoulders?

It is also interesting to note how easy you find it to hold your breath. A person with healthy lungs should be able to hold their breath for at least 30 seconds without difficulty. In my experience, people who have a tendency to over-breathe find this difficult and can often only manage 20, or even as little as ten seconds before they feel compelled to take a breath. Clearly, people with lung conditions would also struggle with holding their breath and so this is no way to differentiate a lung disease from hyperventilation, but if you know you have healthy lungs then it is an interesting observation.

Managing breathing pattern disorders

The first thing to remember is that anything that draws attention to your breathing will tend to make hyperventilation worse, and so if there is any easily reversible condition, such as something as simple as a stuffed-up nose due to hay fever, then it can help to treat it. Or if there is something like asthma working alongside disordered breathing, then make sure this is as well controlled as it can be.

The next step is to really learn about and understand the nature of your breathing. It can help to think about where your disordered breathing pattern may have originated from. It might have started with a panic attack, or generalized anxiety, but it can often follow a more obviously physical illness. Following major surgery, for instance, patients can often be taught to hyperventilate in order to expand their lungs and prevent chest infections, and it can be a hard habit to break once you have got used to it. Or following an episode of COVID, the difficulties some people had with their breathing at the time of the infection can lead to a breathing pattern disorder that hampers their recovery. Clearly, there is a lot more to long COVID than disordered breathing, but it can certainly play a role for some people.

Understanding the explanation for the range of symptoms you are getting can be very helpful in itself. Often when people feel symptoms all over their body, it can feel like they are 'falling apart', as if their body is giving up on them. It's very worrying, and to have an explanation that can bring all the symptoms together can be really helpful. It may be enough to know why you have chest pains, which means you stop worrying about them and so get less anxious and less likely to over-breathe; the vicious cycle has become a virtuous one.

Distraction is an enormously powerful tool when it comes to anxiety in general and disordered breathing in particular, since once we focus on something else, we pay less attention to our breathing and it starts to calm down. When someone is hyperventilating with a panic attack, I often find that they struggle to calm down when I am talking about their breathing or their chest pain, but if I can get them talking about something unrelated, like their work, their home life or the names of their children, then their breathing will often settle without them noticing it.

Finally, and most importantly, you will need to retrain your breathing pattern. The first place to start is to notice how much you breathe through your mouth rather than your nose. Most people with disordered breathing patterns do a lot of mouth breathing, and breathing through our mouths is only helpful when we are exerting ourselves. We can take in a lot of air when we breathe through our mouths, which is helpful when we are running, but it is far less efficient than nasal breathing and tends to make us want to use the muscles in our chest rather than our diaphragm. It is much more instinctive to make sighing breaths when we use our mouths and so simply switching to nasal breathing can make a huge difference. Beyond this, you may want to work with a physiotherapist who has some special expertise in breathing disorders.

I suspect there is a great deal of overlap with how a singing coach would train their pupil, since it is all about restoring the most efficient and effective way to breathe, which is abdominal breathing using your diaphragm rather than your upper chest muscles. The orthodox way for this to work would be for your GP to refer you to a respiratory physiotherapist, but I suspect you could also consider joining a choir and getting some singing lessons.

Chapter 17

Treatments: Cognitive behavioural therapy

A logical solution to a logical problem

A commonly held belief in our society is that you can't fix what's wrong with your body just by talking about it. It isn't a view held by everyone, of course, but it is one I come across quite frequently, and it is a belief that is fundamentally flawed.

I can understand where it is coming from. For starters, there is the assumption that the mind and body are separate, coupled with the stigma we have in our society that diseases of the body are somehow more legitimate than illnesses of the mind; we dread that a doctor might suggest that our physical pain could have a psychological cause, since it implies to us that it is 'all in our head' or that we are making it up. A nice, straightforward, treatable, physical cause for pain is certainly neater and easier to deal with than a psychological explanation.

What is more, talking about how we are feeling is hard; it requires time and commitment and can be emotionally draining. We may have to explore aspects of ourselves that we don't like or remind ourselves of events we prefer to forget. We may even have to be prepared to challenge some of our core beliefs or address our unhelpful behaviours. It is easier to convince ourselves that it cannot work and then we don't have to go there. Or we may have had a bad experience talking about our mental health. We may have opened up to someone who had no way of relating to what we were talking about, since they had no experience of it themselves, or we may have made ourselves vulnerable only to find ourselves being judged. The scars of this often run deep.

Ben felt some of this apprehension before he considered cognitive behavioural therapy (CBT) and we will follow his story.

Ben's story

My anxiety and depression became more obvious in my last year at university. I was one of the top students, but my anxiety made me over-analyse each decision I made in projects. I started to hyper-focus on details – what people might think of each choice I made.

Eventually, I was worrying about everyone's view of me, especially if I didn't know them. I worried people were judging me, to the point that eventually I didn't want to leave my flat. I worried about even going to the corner shop in case I wouldn't have the right change.

I couldn't understand how 'normal' people were able to deal with this 'complex' life. Taxes, contracts, dating… I couldn't even go to buy my shopping without nearly having a breakdown – how can anyone possibly deal with anything more than surviving?

It was scary the first time I went for CBT. I remember my mum dropping me off outside the building and I went in and was ushered into a kitchen where a few others were waiting and told to get a hot drink. Everyone stood against the wall, looking down at their feet. Me included. It was scary.

Ben's experience, which he has kindly allowed me to share here, is not uncommon, both in terms of the overwhelming experience of anxiety and the scary prospect of commencing CBT. He took part in a group-based CBT programme, which can be highly effective, but it is also available working one on one with a therapist. We will come back to Ben's story later and hear how he got on.

Working as a GP, I quickly realized how profoundly and frequently just talking can make a difference to every aspect of a person's life. When I started as a GP, like many young doctors, I wanted to fix every patient I saw. A treatment, a referral, a prescription; they all felt like I was doing something. But I couldn't always think of something *to* do; some problems were not easily fixed, and I often found myself just talking with my patients, unsure of what we were achieving in the appointment.

Just talking didn't always help, but, to my surprise, it often did. Over and over, people would tell me that they felt better just by coming, that they could see the way ahead, or just felt less overwhelmed. And I could see how what people talked about and thought affected what they did, how their bodies responded and, most of all, how they felt. In tapping into this connection between thoughts, feelings and actions, as well as their impact on how our body works, I was doing CBT without even realizing it.

The basis for CBT

The fundamental ideas that underpin CBT are how our thoughts, feelings and actions (or behaviours) interact with each other, each having a significant effect on the other two as well as impacting how our bodies work and the symptoms that might result. The essence of CBT is summed up in Figure 17.1.

How thoughts, feelings and actions impact the body

As we consider how this works, let's first think about how our thoughts, feelings and actions can affect what we notice in our

**Figure 17.1: Thoughts, feelings, actions and our body –
the basis for CBT**

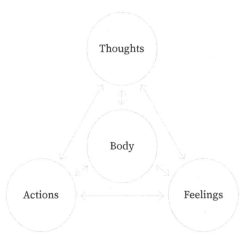

body. We will start with feelings, since if you have been affected by anxiety yourself, you will have no trouble recognizing how the feelings of anxiety can do this. When we are anxious, we get all the physiological effects of adrenaline such as palpitations, tremors, sweaty palms and so on. And so our feelings affect how our body behaves. When we feel calm, our body behaves differently; our heart rate slows, the tension in our shoulders relaxes and so on. What about the other way around? How does our body affect our feelings? Well, that is not hard to see, either, because when our body gives us symptoms, this affects how we feel emotionally. We may feel anxious about those symptoms, or pain might make us feel low, or if our body has pleasurable sensations, we may feel our mood lift or notice a sense of excitement.

It is also easy to see how our body reacts to the actions we choose to take. Taking exercise will change our heart rate and loosen up our muscles, while staying in bed for too long may make our bodies stiff or lethargic. Similarly, our body may give us symptoms that affect the actions we can take; pain may stop us from exercising or a fever may mean we have to stay at home, while feeling pent-up and restless may encourage us to go out for a run.

Perhaps more challenging is to see how our thoughts and beliefs can affect our bodies. At a complex level, what we believe about pain can have a profound impact on the amount of pain we actually feel, but this is hard to see with our own eyes, and it may be simpler to start with something very visual, like blushing. When some people have the thought that they are embarrassed, it causes a very obviously physical response where the blood vessels to their face and upper torso dilate, so that there is an increased blood supply, giving the appearance of blushing. It is involuntary and caused entirely by what the person is thinking. Even more obvious is the way our body responds to thoughts that are sexually arousing.

If our thoughts can affect our physiology in such obvious and profound ways, then why can't what we think and believe affect other physiological processes, such as pain, breathing and bladder and bowel function? Moreover, the way symptoms from our body can impact our thinking is the whole basis for health anxiety, where our beliefs about what our body is telling us tie us entirely in knots!

How thoughts, feelings and actions impact each other

Let's consider how our thoughts, feelings and actions may play off each other. Sometimes it involves the full cycle of thoughts, feelings and actions like this:

- I believe no one likes me and I don't know what to say to people (thoughts) → I feel uncomfortable in social gatherings (feelings) → I avoid going to social gatherings (actions)

→ I get less used to going to social gatherings and so don't get any practice at doing it (actions) → because I am unused to social gatherings, I believe no one likes me and I don't know what to say to people (thoughts) → I feel uncomfortable in social gatherings (feelings).

Or sometimes it involves only two aspects bouncing off one another:

- I feel low and miserable (feelings) → I am too low to open the curtains and so stay inside in the dark (actions) → being cooped up like this makes me feel low and miserable (feelings).
- I believe I am a rubbish person (thoughts) → I feel really low as I know how rubbish I am (feelings) → I feel so low that I think I'd rather I wasn't here (thoughts).

CBT is all about recognizing these patterns, working out which ones are happening for you and figuring out where you can make changes that will be helpful. You can do CBT on your own, but it can be really helpful to work with someone who is used to how this works and can help you explore what is happening in your life. This is where working with a therapist can make such a difference, as they can help you gain insights that lead to real change.

Feelings are subjective and cannot be challenged

When it comes to thoughts, feelings and actions, feelings tend to dominate. They are immediate and demand our constant attention. They are what we feel here and now, and not what we might feel tomorrow or what we felt yesterday. They only live in the present and they *cannot* be challenged. What I mean by this is that if you are feeling low, sad or anxious, then you cannot just tell yourself to feel better. You feel what you feel. No one can tell you that you don't feel it, and telling yourself to simply feel something else really doesn't work. This is why telling someone to cheer up or be happy is ineffectual. A feeling cannot be false; it just is what it is, and it is what it feels like to you that matters – this is why they are both subjective and unchallengeable.

Feelings can usually be described in a single word, like 'happy' or 'sad' or 'anxious' or 'angry' or 'hopeless'. One thing that is confusing about the English language is that we often use the word 'feel' when we mean 'believe'; we might say, 'I feel that I have let everyone down', but this is describing a thought or a belief and not a feeling. We might feel sad, or regretful, or depressed because we believe we have let everyone down. If ever you find yourself using more than one word to describe what you feel, you are probably describing your thoughts and not your feelings. This is important because thoughts *can* be challenged in a way that you can't challenge a feeling.

Feelings want to be in charge, but they are a poor leader

Feelings can be positive as well as negative, but when they are unpleasant, they have a tendency to want to be in charge. They grab our attention and won't let go, and the more distressing they are, the more they demand that we deal with them, urgently. But they are a poor leader. This is because they are only focused on the present and have little regard for the future or memory of the past. When we are feeling overwhelmed with sadness, it is hard to remember that we felt happy yesterday. When we are struggling with the feeling of anxiety, it is easy to forget that this is because we usually feel anxious in the mornings, and hard to remember that it is often much better once we get to the afternoon. All we can focus on is how unpleasant these feelings are and how we want to get rid of these feelings now.

There is nothing wrong with wanting to feel better, but what is key is how these feelings influence our thoughts and actions, and how we need to be in charge of our thoughts and actions and not allow our feelings to control things. Sometimes feelings might guide us to the right action; we might feel sad that we have upset someone, and our feelings lead us to an appropriate apology, but at other times we might feel sad and apologize when we have nothing to apologize for, and our feelings might simply keep us trapped in a toxic relationship. Sometimes we might feel tense, and this feeling leads to going out for a run, which is helpful, but the feeling of tension might also lead to drinking too much alcohol, comfort eating or self-harming, all of which are unhelpful actions.

Most often, our feelings are behind the cycle of avoidance that makes anxiety so much worse. The whole of CBT, and even the whole of this book, could be summed up by the need to manage our feelings by getting our thinking in order and choosing helpful actions, rather than allowing our thoughts and actions to be the unquestioning servants of our feelings.

Challenge your thoughts

Whereas our feelings cannot be challenged, the most useful and important thing to do with negative thoughts is to question and challenge them. You may have the thought, for instance, that you are no good at making friends. Often our thoughts will seem absolute and unchallengeable, and we will find ourselves using words like 'can't' or 'don't'; you might think to yourself, 'I can't make friends,' or, 'I don't do parties.' These words make these beliefs seem stronger than they are, but these statements are open to challenge. What is the evidence that you can't make friends? Do you have anyone who would call you a friend? If so, what does that say about the statement that you can't make friends? What would one of your friends say about whether or not you can make friends? If one of your friends said that they couldn't make friends, what would you say to them? If you could challenge their thoughts, can you also challenge your own? Sometimes it is worth imagining putting your thoughts in the dock; how would they stand up under questioning?

When we start to challenge our thoughts like this, then we open the door to being able to think differently. We need to be realistic; you will probably still conclude that you find it difficult to make friends, but you have started the process of thinking differently, and as your thoughts change, so your feelings will change with them. Once you remind yourself that you do have some friends, you will feel a little less bad and a little less lonely. You can work with that. The thoughts you need to challenge may be very different to the example above.

Other examples of unhelpful thoughts that might need to be challenged are:

- 'I am a bad person.'
- 'I can't reduce my commitments because everyone relies on me so much.'
- 'I can't ever forgive.'
- 'I won't ever get better.'
- 'When I think there is anything wrong with my body, I must always check it out with a doctor.'
- 'I can't control my anger.'

It may be that you find this extremely difficult: that you try to challenge your thoughts, but no matter how compelling the evidence ought to be, your brain just won't be convinced – it behaves like a biased jury that will never be swayed by the arguments because it has already made up its mind!

This is certainly one criticism of CBT: that for some people it is just too difficult to challenge their thoughts. If this is you, then you might be better to take a step further back, so that instead of challenging the content of your thoughts, you examine the effect that thinking in this way is having on your life. So, for instance, instead of trying to convince yourself that you can make friends, you recognize that you are having negative thoughts about your ability to make friends and examine the impact of spending time thinking in this way.

Even if you find that you can challenge your thoughts, you may feel overwhelmed by how many thoughts there are for you to work on! This is why CBT is hard to do on your own and why working with a therapist can be so helpful. They won't tell you what to do, but they will help you to gain insight into what you could do that would help. The best solutions are always the ones you work out for yourself, but sometimes a therapist, or a doctor, can be an important catalyst to help you get there.

Choose your actions

The most important parts of CBT, which we have full control of, are the actions we take and the choices we make. As we have said, we can't just tell ourselves to feel better, and challenging beliefs can be difficult and take time, but we can always choose a better action. And the remarkable thing about our actions is the effect they can have on our feelings. This is why our feelings always try to get us to take actions that will make us feel better, and feel better quickly. This is the reason we are tempted to avoid anything that makes us anxious, have a drink, comfort eat, restrict our eating, perform a ritual and so on. Each time the distressing feeling we are subjected to tries to get us to take an action that will bring relief as quickly and completely as possible. This is why it is so easy to get into the habit of unhealthy, destructive actions that help in the short term and have a long-term cost.

However, we can use this understanding of how actions affect feelings in a much more positive way. Once we understand what actions help us to feel better, and build a repertoire of healthy actions that we can rely upon, then we are in charge and our feelings will fall into line, responding to the action we have taken.

We all see this in everyday life. When I am feeling stressed and wound up, for example, I will often head out into the garden for half an hour. The combination of being outdoors, physical exercise and distraction makes a huge difference. By the time I finish, the problem I was worrying about may not have changed, but my attitude towards it is in a different place. I have stopped ruminating on it, my mind has been thinking of other things, my body feels better for the activity and, lo and behold, *I feel better*.

What is really important is that I did not wait until I *felt* like gardening. Had I waited until I felt like doing it, then it might have got dark before I made it outside. My feelings were elsewhere, in whatever I was feeling tense about, but I have enough insight into what makes me feel good to know that I needed to go outside, and that it would help.

For you, it might be different actions that help. It might be going for a run or to the gym, or maybe seeing a friend or phoning your mum. It might be doing cross-stitch, tackling a crossword or baking, or possibly just a simple action of putting your phone down or having a bath. It might be choosing to stop looking at unhelpful websites or choosing to read a helpful book, deciding to have a night without alcohol or a night with healthier food. It could be picking up the phone and saying sorry to a good friend or picking up the phone and blocking the number of a bad one. It could be filling in an online form on your doctor's website to ask for help, calling the crisis line, asking to be signed off work or taking the dog for a walk.

The importance of agency

We are faced with choices every day and throughout every day. Some are small choices and others are big life events, and we need to realize that we do have a say in all of them. In her powerful and haunting book *The Choice*,[10] Holocaust survivor and psychologist Edith Eger talks about how, while we are still living, we always have some control over the choices we make. At one stage in her life, when reduced to eating grass to stay alive, she was struck that, even then, she could still choose which blade of grass to pick. Had this been written by someone who had not been through the suffering she had endured, then it would sound like trite nonsense, but the point she was making is not that she was glad to be reduced to such a pathetic choice, but the importance of agency – of having a say in the choices we make – because it is this agency that gives us an active say in our future.

Stigma against mental illness, and the blame culture that comes with it, is gradually becoming less of an issue. While there is still ignorance out there, we no longer blame people for becoming mentally unwell. This is absolutely right – the causes of mental illness are complex and often outside our control – but there is an opposite danger to blame, which is passivity. If I am not to blame for being unwell, then that can lead to the conclusion that I have no say in my health and that my mental illness is all the result of external factors over which I have no control. This passivity, and the psychology of victimhood that can result, will impede recovery. The first step to getting well may be to regain a sense of agency, and a belief that you can have a say in the choices you make, and that sometimes even a seemingly small change in those choices can start to make a difference.

Building a repertoire of healthy actions

We don't have to be at the mercy of our feelings, but we *can* make our feelings better by making the right choices. It helps if we can build a repertoire of different actions we can take that we know are helpful for managing our anxiety. My go-to preference for gardening as a stress reliever won't help me when it is dark or raining, and the feel-good effect of having a cat sit on my lap won't help when I am in the office. We need different strategies for different situations and in different time frames. We need to balance them with the demands of our life, so that we have enough time to do healthy activities while also recognizing that we have other activities that just have to be done, like putting food on the table, doing the shopping, picking the children up from school and so on. Even here, though, ordinary, everyday activities can be helpful, since one of the core principles behind any action that can help with difficult feelings is the value of distraction.

Distraction is such a powerful tool for helping with anxiety for the simple reason that we struggle to focus on more than one thing at once. When we are worrying about something, it often dominates our thoughts, and we often can't manage to think ourselves out of worrying about it. We can challenge our thoughts, and this can help to some extent, but then we are still thinking about it and probably still worrying about it. The best way to stop thinking about something is to displace those thoughts with something else. Even something as banal as making the dinner or cleaning the kitchen floor can often give us something new to think about, and, before long, we discover that our thoughts have moved on. We didn't notice when we stopped thinking about the cause of our worry; we just moved on, our feelings obediently followed and now we feel a bit better.

Let's get back to hear how Ben got on.

Ben's experience

The course was two hours with homework. I still have all the paperwork we were given to remind me how far I've come, as we had to rate how anxious we felt and at what points in our day.

After four weeks, I could already see a light. They told us how our brains were perceiving normal activities as dangers. The fight-or-flight response was being set off by more and more things and would take anything it could as confirmation and never saw the positives as counters to that.

So they forced us to try to push a little out of our comfort. Not too far, but enough that we were a bit anxious.

I remember thinking that I hoped CBT wouldn't be something I would have to consciously do day in, day out, because that would be just as bad as dealing with my anxiety. But it just became how my brain worked. It stopped being a conscious thing after a few months. It just became how I thought.

CBT saved my life, and that's not hyperbole; I honestly don't know if I'd be here right now as life felt too hard for me. Now I still have nervous moments, but not anxiety on the levels I used to have. I haven't had a panic attack since 2013.

CBT gave me skills that I think everyone should have for dealing with worries.

CBT and other talking therapies

CBT is not the only talking therapy out there, but I have focused on it as it is the most common type of therapy available and can be particularly helpful when it comes to anxiety. Other talking therapies may be better at exploring complex issues from your past, or dealing with relationship issues, trauma or bereavement, although there is a great deal of overlap between different approaches. People sometimes ask me if they need talking therapy, and I usually say to them that this is the wrong question. It is not about whether or not you *need* it, as though you have to be bad enough to deserve it, but a question of whether it would help. And if it would help, then are you ready to put in the time and effort it will require?

It might be that you want to go for therapy, but your brain is so frazzled that you are not sure you will be able to focus on it and put it into practice, which is one reason why you might want to consider medication, an important topic that we will consider next.

Chapter 18

Treatments: Medication

Not for everyone, but it has its place

A search on the internet for 'antidepressant tabloid headlines' quickly yields the sort of results that doctors dread, knowing the impact that the latest flavour of news could have on their coming week. One day, the headline confidently informs us that we would all feel better if we took antidepressants, and that many more people should be on them; the following week, we are condemned for being a nation hooked on happy pills! While I am confident that most people are too savvy to take much notice of sensational tabloid headlines, it does contribute to the mythology around antidepressant medication, which can make it so hard to navigate this topic!

What's in a name?

One confusing aspect about the group of medications that have the biggest role in treating all forms of anxiety is something I cannot blame the tabloids for: despite being used as often for anxiety as for depression, they are all called antidepressants! It is so unhelpful when I am talking to a patient about treating their anxiety and I am faced with completely the wrong word! 'But I'm not depressed!' is the obvious response I can expect when I try to recommend an antidepressant. We can usually find a way around the semantics and get through this obstacle, but – just to be clear – antidepressants really are as much a treatment for anxiety as they are for depression.

Is there something I could take when I feel I need it?

The most obvious pill to hope for when you are affected by anxiety is something you could take at the time when you feel anxious that would help you to feel calmer. There is a lot that seems attractive about such an idea. The awful feelings of anxiety are what makes it so unpleasant, after all, so the idea of having something to take those feelings away sounds fantastic. What is more, it seems better than being on a daily pill, since you would only take it on an 'as needed' basis. In terms of 'being on medication', this doesn't sound so bad as you are not really on it; you only have it there just in case.

For these reasons, I can fully understand why so many people ask me if they can have an 'as needed' pill for their anxiety, and I always feel I have to let them down when I explain why there are real problems with this approach.

The first issue is nothing to do with the actual medication that we could consider, and it is the idea of using a pill of any sort to calm anxiety. The problem with taking a pill to settle anxiety there and then is that it does not empower you in any way. You may feel calmer after taking it, but that is because of the effect of a drug and not because you have learned anything about yourself or improved your skills at managing and facing your fear. You may have been able to do something you have been avoiding, but only through the effects of medication. I suppose if there were a tablet that really worked for anxiety, and had no short- or long-term downsides, then maybe it wouldn't matter if you always had to take one whenever you felt anxious. The problem is, there are other downsides to these tablets.

There are two medications that are sometimes prescribed on an 'as needed' basis – beta-blockers and benzodiazepines – and we will consider both. The first works on our body's response to anxiety while the second works on our central nervous system.

Beta-blockers

Beta-blockers are so called because they block the beta-receptors that are responsible for many of the effects of adrenaline. They are mostly used for treating heart conditions and high blood pressure, but one called propranolol is a treatment for migraine and is sometimes used for anxiety.

Adrenaline is produced in the adrenal gland and has an effect on the cells in the body by binding to receptors on the cells; there are both alpha- and beta-receptors, but when it comes to the symptoms we feel when we are anxious, such as a racing heart, trembling, feeling sick and a lump in the throat, it is the beta-receptors that matter. Beta-blockers bind to these receptors and get in the way of the adrenaline, so reducing its effect. In this way, beta-blockers don't have any direct effects on the brain, so they don't make you feel calmer in your head, they just reduce your body's response to the fear; your heart doesn't race quite as much, your stomach doesn't have quite so many butterflies and so on. This can be helpful and so GPs do sometimes prescribe them, but the benefits are limited and there are several caveats:

- Most importantly, they are not recommended for the treatment of anxiety, at least in the UK. Although it is not uncommon for them to be prescribed, there is no mention of beta-blockers in the guidance for generalized anxiety disorder produced by the National Institute for Health and Care Excellence (NICE),[11] which all doctors in the UK follow. Doctors are not told *not* to prescribe them; there is just no mention of them. The reason for this is that the evidence that they make any real, lasting difference is distinctly lacking.

- In practice, although some patients seem to find them helpful, the benefit is usually small and they only help there and then, so do not deal with the underlying issues of anxiety or have any longer-term benefits.

- There are reasons why some people should not take beta-blockers, with the most important being asthma. People with asthma will be familiar with their 'reliever' medication, which is a beta-agonist: *the exact opposite* of a beta-blocker. And so it is easy to see how a beta-blocker could cause asthma to get worse – if ever you feel wheezy on a beta-blocker, you should seek urgent medical advice.

- As well as stopping the heart from going too fast when you feel anxious, beta-blockers also slow the heart rate when you are at rest and doing normal activities, which can lower your blood pressure and cause dizziness. If you take a beta-blocker for some time, and so have got used to a slow pulse, it can take some getting used to having a faster heart rate again when you stop using it!

Benzodiazepines

Benzodiazepines are the classic sleeping tablet, with the most common examples being diazepam (Valium), temazepam and nitrazepam, while alprazolam has become notorious in the US under the tradename Xanax. I always feel that the very worst thing about benzodiazepines is that they work so well! That sounds odd, but what I mean by this is that they are highly sedating, and so the feelings of anxiety are quickly calmed in the very short term. This can make them very appealing, but ignores their major downside, which is how addictive they are. In a very short space of time, if benzodiazepines are taken regularly, the body becomes tolerant to them, and then dependent on them. Tolerance means they become less effective over time, with bigger and bigger doses needed to get the same effect, while dependence means that withdrawal symptoms, including worsening anxiety, occur when doses are reduced or stopped.

This class of drug should be used with caution, therefore. They definitely have a role in very short-term anxiety – for instance, to help someone overcome claustrophobia so that they can have an MRI scan – or for very short-term use in severe mental illness, but ideally we would not use them. Diazepam often used to be prescribed for flying phobia, but, due to the risks associated with its sedative nature, this is now no longer recommended. And, as they are sedating, you cannot drive after taking them.

I'm sorry, I've not been very encouraging about medication so far!

SSRI antidepressants

One class of medication that definitely has a role in the treatment of both anxiety and burnout is the selective serotonin reuptake inhibitors (SSRIs), which are the main class of modern medication usually referred to as antidepressants. The main medications in this class are sertraline, citalopram and fluoxetine.

How do they work? To be honest, we don't really know! They block the reuptake of an important chemical, serotonin, which increases its effect (hence the name). We know that serotonin helps nerves to communicate with each other and, when we block its reuptake, that stops it from being removed from where it operates, so it hangs around longer and thereby is more effective. What is less clear is what this has to do with anxiety or depression. The idea that people with these conditions were in some way lacking this chemical used to be an orthodox belief but is now very much in question.

What we *do* know, however, is that they *do* work. We have good scientific studies that prove they can have a positive impact on both anxiety and depression, and since they have been around for well over 30 years, we have a very good understanding of what to expect from them, which side effects to look out for and so on. This is good enough for me. If I were a scientist, I would want to know the exact

neuroscience behind how and why they work, but as a doctor or a patient, I just want to know that they do work, what to expect when I prescribe them and what the side effects might be!

What should you expect if you were to try them? In his book *Depressive Illness: The Curse of the Strong* (which I referenced in Chapter 8), Dr Tim Cantopher uses the brilliant analogy of an empty bath. The tap is running, but the plug is out and all the water has drained away. That, he says, is how you are when you are affected by anxiety, burnout or depression: drained away. It's an analogy that works, since that is exactly how you feel. Taking an antidepressant is like putting the plug in, and the bath takes four to six weeks to fill. This is a tremendously helpful image, since it is obvious that it is not the plug that makes a bath feel good, it is the water filling the bath up. The expectation that you won't feel better immediately after you start the medication is built into the image you are left with.

Here is what I tell my patients to expect:

- It usually takes two to six weeks to start feeling any benefit from the medication; if you feel any improvement in the first two weeks, that is a bonus.
- You may get some temporary side effects when you first start them. Nausea and light-headedness are the most common and they are usually mild. Sometimes a temporary increase in anxiety can also occur. These should settle within a week, certainly within two weeks. These symptoms can also occur when you first stop taking them, which is why you can feel a bit weird if you miss tablets. If someone is worried about these side effects, then they are less likely to get them by increasing the tablet in small steps, and reducing in small steps when stopping them.

- Longer-term side effects can occur, with the most important ones being the possibility of weight gain and sexual dysfunction. Weight gain can happen as these tablets sometimes make people more hungry, so the key thing is to check that this doesn't result in eating more than usual. On the sexual side, anxiety and depression may both have a negative impact here, so taking medication may actually improve things, but in some cases, there can be a loss of sex drive or difficulty with erections and it is important to know this can happen. Usually, it is temporary, but there are cases of it being very prolonged after treatment has stopped (a condition called post-SSRI sexual dysfunction or PSSD).

- There is also a very rare, but potentially very serious reaction to these drugs called serotonin syndrome, which occurs soon after taking them and can make someone very unwell, with confusion, agitation, sweating and muscular twitching. It's important that people are aware of this when they start taking them as they must stop them and seek urgent medical advice, but it is incredibly rare.

- It is important not to stop them too soon (you don't want to take the plug out of the bath as soon as you have filled it up!) and so, if we are happy that they are working, then I would usually expect someone to stay on them for at least six months.

Aren't they just masking things?

Well, maybe, but that can still be very helpful. Listening to the experience of my patients, they often tell me that they don't notice anything at first, but around three weeks they start to feel calmer and to feel their mood lift, and by six weeks things are really improving. Not everyone finds them helpful, of course, and sometimes it takes a while to work out the right dose, or even the right SSRI, but there is improvement more often than not. People will often tell me that they just don't feel frightened as much as before, or the instinct to react impulsively in an unhelpful way has calmed down. Is this masking their symptoms or curing the problem? It's hard to say!

What I can say is that if I try to treat someone's anxiety with an SSRI but make no changes to their understanding of anxiety to equip them with the tools for how to manage it, then I am doing them no favours. Similarly, if I prescribe an SSRI to someone who is affected by burnout, but we do nothing to reduce the pressure they are under, then we are simply papering over the cracks, and at best they will only delay the full effect of their illness. On the other hand, sometimes the symptoms of anxiety are so bad that it is impossible to contemplate therapy. We need to reduce those symptoms with an SSRI first, so that they can then engage in the therapy which will be their real treatment. Or another person may be signed off work with burnout, but their symptoms are so distressing that a little bit of masking those symptoms would be very welcome, thank you very much!

The key thing is that these tablets are not addictive and may open the door to the therapy or life changes that will keep someone well, once they have got out of the initial rut they are in. And some people will find they are best to stay on such medication long-term; are they masking it or keeping it in remission? Maybe when the choice is being well and thriving or being unwell and struggling, this is a distinction that doesn't really matter!

The stigma of medication for mental illness

It deeply saddens me that there is stigma around the use of medication in mental illness in a way that doesn't exist for physical health problems, such as diabetes, asthma or cancer. This can be from others, who see it as weakness to use medication, or have had a bad personal experience with antidepressants that they use to frighten others considering them, or have conspiratorial ideas that medications designed to work on the brain must have sinister connotations. I see this whenever I post on social media about medication for mental illness; most of the comments are supportive and helpful, but there will always be one or two very unhelpful comments making wild generalizations about these drugs and the wicked GPs who prescribe them!

Perhaps more damaging, though, are the prejudices we may have ourselves towards taking medication. It is very reasonable in most medical contexts to look at non-drug treatments before putting any sort of chemical in our body, but the internal resistance to taking antidepressants can sometimes be out of proportion and we can be overly judgemental on ourselves when we consider taking them. Taking medication is not a sign of weakness or an admission that we lack the moral fibre to get better on our own; all that matters is a considered opinion of whether or not this is the right treatment to consider at the moment, and enough understanding to weigh the benefits and potential side effects of trying them.

Will I be 'drugged up' if I take them?

This is a reasonable concern to have, and the answer is a very clear 'no'; SSRIs are not sedating and you will not feel 'drugged up' when you are on them (although one similar medication called mirtazapine is sedating and so is taken at night, usually prescribed when sleep is a problem). What people sometimes describe for me, though, is that while they feel entirely their normal self most of the time, they don't quite react in the same way they used to at the extremes of their emotional range. They report that they don't cry when watching a sad movie or feel as excited as usual when they get good news. The best analogy I can think of is that they are like a piano keyboard where all the middle notes are working normally, but they can't quite hit the very lowest or the very highest notes. At first, this is usually welcome, since not crying every time they go to the supermarket is a clear win, but in time people sometimes tell me they are ready to have the full range of their emotions back. This is often a good sign that they are ready to reduce the dose, or even come off them completely.

When to stop an antidepressant

I usually ask my patients four key questions when we are considering reducing the dose of an antidepressant:

- **Have you been well for at least four months?** We look back and ask when they started to feel well. If this is within the last four months, then it may be too early to reduce, but if it has been four months or more, then that is a good sign.
- **Is there a major life event coming up?** There will always be stresses on the horizon, so we should not be too timid on this one, but making a change just before a major life event, like starting a new job, retiring, moving house, having a child or getting married, is usually a bad idea!
- **Has something changed that gives us reason to think you won't just get ill again?** This one is really key. The change may be that someone has had a period of therapy and has acquired new skills to manage their anxiety or reduce the risk of burnout, or it might be a change in circumstance; perhaps the work environment has improved, or a relationship difficulty has resolved, or enough time has passed

since a traumatic life event that healing has occurred. Put simply, this question is: how optimistic can we be that you won't get sick again?

- **Is it the right time of year for you?** This is a very personal one and will depend on the country you live in and your circumstances. In the UK, with cold, damp and dark winters, most people find the winter more of a struggle, and the best time of year to consider coming off medication is the spring, with the weather warming and the days getting longer. Some people are the other way around, however, and love the cosiness of winter and feel their mood drop when the temperatures rise. Or it may have nothing to do with the seasons and it is the rhythm of a busy season at work you need to take note of, or the timing of important anniversaries.

If the answers to all four questions are encouraging, then we are usually ready to come off medication, often in a stepped way so that we don't stop them all at once.

Make sure you speak to your doctor

Clearly, a chapter on medication can only cover general principles. The exact nature of any treatment you may want to try will need to be specifically tailored to you in discussion with your doctor. Your past medical history, other prescribed medication and previous experience with tablets will all play a crucial role in deciding what medication to take. And when it comes to antidepressants, SSRIs are only one class; there are SNRIs, atypical antidepressants, TCAs, serotonin modulators and even MAOIs to contend with, but, for most of these, I would need to look up the acronym to remind myself what it stood for – and would ask a psychiatrist for advice before prescribing them!

Conclusion

I started this book by saying how anxiety can often leave us feeling foolish. I hope by now you agree with me that there is nothing foolish about being anxious: your worry really does make sense! Or, if you are reading this book to help care for someone else with anxiety, that their worry makes sense; they are not being irrational, awkward or unreasonable, and it is not something they can just snap out of. If you've ever found yourself saying to someone with anxiety, 'But you've nothing to be worried about,' or said these same words to yourself in a state of exasperation, then hopefully by now you will understand just how off the mark you were.

Be kind to yourself, though – it is natural to think that anxiety should be closely related to 'having something to worry about', when in reality it is more a pattern of thinking; it will *always* find something to worry about, and if there is nothing obvious to worry about, then it will worry about *not* having something to worry about!

There is nothing ridiculous about anxiety, just as there is nothing weak about burnout, but both can take us by surprise and lead us to unhelpful patterns of thinking and unhelpful behaviours that, at best, hamper our recovery and, at worst, leave us in an ever-tightening cycle that dominates our lives. There is so much that can be done to help, though; we really can loosen the ties of anxiety and start to experience freedom from fear, and we really can challenge our thinking, so that we not only recover from burnout, but learn to prevent it in the first place.

And this is the crunch point, where the rubber hits the road and the only question that really matters is this: what are you going to do now? There is nothing foolish about anxiety but if, having read this far, and knowing that anxiety or burnout are real issues for you; if, having understood some of what can be done, and having learned that the power is in your hands to start the process of change; if, then, at this point, you chose to do nothing, then maybe that really would be foolish.

It would be understandable to do nothing, since deciding to push even slightly beyond your comfort zone is both scary and hard work. It will not be easy to redefine yourself so that you no longer see yourself as the anxious one, to imagine what it would be like to be free of anxiety, to function again without being scared, to catch your brain thinking without fear. What would that be like? It might feel scary to take the risk of teaching your brain how not to be on high-threat alert all the time; you would have to decide that the threat level is not what your brain would have you believe. If you managed to turn the threat level down, you might find yourself feeling calm, and even that can be so unfamiliar as to be scary! There is something comforting about the familiar, even if it is an anxious way of being that you don't like and want to change.

It would be understandable to do nothing, but it would be a shame, since there is so much that can be done to help. So, what might you do? It may be that you choose to go back to Chapter 12 and start putting small, achievable plans in place for your anxiety rehabilitation; or perhaps you will tap into some right-brain activities and put them into your regular routine for your wellbeing; or maybe sleep is an issue and you will change the setting on your alarm clock and start working on some of those marginal gains; or perhaps you need to learn how to let go, or how to say no.

You might be really motivated at this point, but make sure any goals you set are realistic and achievable; don't bite off more than you can chew and end up berating yourself when you fall over. Take it one small step at a time and ask yourself if this is something you are going to do on your own, or if you are going to get someone to help you. This might be a close friend or family member who helps you set and achieve your goals as you expand your comfort zone into your expansion zone, or it might be that you would do well to work with a therapist first.

I sometimes have patients say to me, 'I've tried CBT, it didn't work.' I often ask them what they mean. What do they mean by 'it' and 'not working'? It's the sort of language we might use with a simple problem in the home, like 'I tried changing the fuse, but it didn't work' or 'I turned it off and on again but it still didn't work.' The 'it' is a one-off action, and we are unable to influence whether or not it works; it was just something to try out. CBT, or any talking therapy, is so much more than that. It is not something to passively receive and see if it works or not, but a process to be actively engaged in. And when it comes to 'working' or not, it is far from a binary 'yes it worked' or 'no it didn't'; it can have a whole range of benefits and some may take a while to become apparent.

When someone says to me that CBT didn't work, I always wonder what went wrong. Perhaps they weren't prepared for the therapy at the time. Maybe they were dragged into it by someone else who thought it would do them good and they were never convinced, or maybe they didn't have the time or emotional energy to engage in the therapy, or perhaps they just didn't connect with the therapist they met up with and would do much better with a different therapist? Sometimes CBT isn't the right approach. For someone who is neurodivergent, for instance, CBT would need to be adapted to suit a person with autism, while an alternative therapy such as acceptance and commitment therapy (ACT; a therapy based on CBT but with a more holistic approach) might suit some people when standard CBT has not seemed the right fit.

Whatever type of therapy you might consider, if you are going to work with a therapist, it will take time and commitment, and so you need to be at the point where you feel able to give these on both a practical and emotional level. In order to get the best out of it, it needs to be grabbed with both hands and an attitude that says 'I don't like the way anxiety is affecting me right now, so I'm going to put effort into this and I'm going to extract every last piece of benefit and learning that I can.'

And I think this gets me to the final point I want to make, which is this: you have to be sufficiently *annoyed* with your anxiety to make the changes that will make a difference. And by your anxiety, I don't mean the anxiety itself, since hating anxiety is what drives people to avoid anything that makes them anxious. I mean that you should be *annoyed by the restrictions anxiety is placing on your life*. If you are not annoyed by this, then you won't have the energy to make the changes that will start to set you free. And maybe that's okay, because maybe anxiety is not having that big an impact and you can easily live with it. But if anxiety is dominating your life, then let those limitations annoy you and allow them to frustrate you enough that you are ready for change. You don't have to fight the anxiety itself; in fact, accepting your anxiety and learning to laugh with it may be just the way to start change, but you do need to *want* to change, and in this regard, a little bit of annoyance can go a long way!

About the author

Dr Martin Brunet is a general practitioner working in the UK near Guildford. He has been at his practice since qualifying as a GP in 2001 and has always taken an interest in training and medical education. Alongside his work as an NHS GP, he works as a freelance speaker, educator and writer. His interest in how doctors communicate with their patients led to the publication of his first book, *The GP Consultation Reimagined: A Tale of Two Houses* in 2020.

Martin's interest in both education and mental health have come together in recent years, fuelling a passion for helping patients to understand what is happening to them with their mental health, leading to a significant profile on social media where he posts regularly as Doc Martin GP on topics connected to mental health.

You can find Martin on social media here:

 Instagram
@doc_martin_gp

 TikTok
@doc_martin_gp

Endnotes

1 Martel, Y. (2001) *Life of Pi*. Canongate Books, p.161.
2 Hall, C. (2019) 'Can anything cure my lifelong fear of cotton wool?' *The Guardian*, 10 November. www.theguardian.com/society/2019/nov/10/cotton-wool-thinking-can-i-conquer-my-unusual-phobia-buttons-bananas
3 Peanuts by Charles Schulz, 27 February 1963. GoComics. www.gocomics.com/peanuts/1963/02/27
4 Martel, Y. (2001) *Life of Pi*. Canongate Books, p.161.
5 Prochaska, J.O. and DiClemente, C.C. (1983) 'Stages and processes of self-change of smoking: Toward an integrative model of change.' *Journal of Consulting and Clinical Psychology 51*, 3, 390–395.
6 National Institute for Health and Care Excellence (2014) *Anxiety Disorders* [QS53]. www.nice.org.uk/guidance/qs53
7 Cantopher, T. (2012) *Depressive Illness: The Curse of the Strong*. Sheldon Press.
8 Maurer, L.F., Schneider, J., Miller, C.B., Espie, C.A. and Kyle, S.D. (2021) 'The clinical effects of sleep restriction therapy for insomnia: A meta-analysis of randomised controlled trials.' *Sleep Medicine Reviews 58*, 101493 (2021).
9 Miller, C.B., Espie, C.A., Epstein, D.R., Friedman, L. *et al.* (2014) 'The evidence base of sleep restriction therapy for treating insomnia disorder.' *Sleep Medicine Reviews 18*, 5, 415–424.
10 Eger, E. (2018) *The Choice*. Rider Books.
11 National Institute for Health and Care Excellence (2020) *Generalised Anxiety Disorder and Panic Disorder in Adults: Management* [CG113]. www.nice.org.uk/guidance/cg113

Notes